MIRACLE MOMENTS
IN
ALABAMA CRIMSON TIDE
FOOTBALL HISTORY

BEST PLAYS, GAMES, AND RECORDS

MARK MAYFIELD

SPORTS
PUBLISHING

Sports Publishing books may be purchased in bulk at special discounts for sales promotion, corporate gifts, fund-raising, or educational purposes. Special editions can also be created to specifications. For details, contact the Special Sales Department, Sports Publishing, 307 West 36th Street, 11th Floor, New York, NY 10018 or sportspubbooks@skyhorsepublishing.com.

Sports Publishing® is a registered trademark of Skyhorse Publishing, Inc.®, a Delaware corporation.

Visit our website at www.sportspubbooks.com.

10 9 8 7 6 5 4 3 2 1

Library of Congress Cataloging-in-Publication Data is available on file.

Cover design by Tom Lau
Cover photo credit: Associated Press

ISBN: 978-1-68358-186-4
Ebook ISBN: 978-1-68358-188-8

Printed in China

Contents

Part Two: Remember the Rose Bowl: Alabama Goes National

Part Three: The Epic Era of Paul "Bear" Bryant

Part Four: Glimpses of Past Glory: Alabama in the Post-Bryant Era

Part Five: A Modern Dynasty: Nick Saban's Crimson Tide

Dedication

For Dewey and Phyllis Mayfield, who have taught by example, led exemplary lives, and always been there with their support. Nobody ever had better parents. And for Larry, gone far too soon, but brothers are forever. My, how he would love what Nick Saban has accomplished in Tuscaloosa. Roll Tide.

Introduction:
A Championship Legacy

When Tua Tagovailoa launched a perfect 41-yard strike to DeVonta Smith to win the 2018 College Football Playoff national championship game in overtime, both players instantly became part of something even larger than such a dazzling moment.

The walk-off touchdown between the two sensational freshmen on a January night in Atlanta gave the Alabama Crimson Tide a thrilling 26–23 victory over Georgia and secured an unprecedented fifth national championship in nine years. In short, it added another chapter to the story of the greatest dynasty college football has ever seen.

DeVonta Smith celebrates his winning touchdown in the 2018 CFP National Championship Game. (Photo by Sam MacDonald/*The Crimson White*, courtesy of the UA Office of Student Media)

For the packed crowd who witnessed it firsthand in Mercedes-Benz Stadium, and the millions who watched it on television, via 124 cameras ESPN trained on every aspect of the game, it was a jaw-dropping end to a classic championship contest.

Yet, for Alabama's players, coaches, and fans, it was not just another title, or a singular moment in time. It added to the rich lore of one of America's greatest sports programs. Nick Saban and his Alabama teams have reached extraordinary levels of accomplishment in the past decade. And given the challenges with modern scholarship limitations, intense recruiting wars, and a playoff, their championships are even more remarkable. Yet, they have also inherited, and greatly built upon, a grand tradition of winning that stretches back more than a century.

From the afternoon a group of young men from The University of Alabama in Tuscaloosa stepped onto a baseball field in Birmingham in 1892 and played their first game of "foot ball" in front of a handful of onlookers, to the night Tagovailoa, Smith, and their teammates won that thriller in Atlanta on January 8, 2018, this team and this program have been something special.

If this were a Hollywood script, it would begin—appropriately enough—in Pasadena, California, on January 1, 1926, when two of the best football players in the nation, Allison "Pooley" Hubert and future movie star Johnny Mack Brown, led Alabama to an earth-shattering 20–19 upset of heavily-favored Washington in the Rose Bowl. Though the Crimson Tide had won some important battles before—including a landmark 1922 road win over then-college football power Penn in Philadelphia—the curtain truly went up for Alabama and the entirety of southern football on that New Year's Day in Pasadena.

"It was considered by many to be the worst mismatch in the history of the game. Alabama had a good enough record—nine straight wins—but football experts in the '20s all knew that southern football was barely on a level with junior varsity play in the rest of the country," began a 1962 story in *Sports Illustrated*, recapping the monumental significance of the game 36 years earlier. "As it turned out, Alabama won—in the most thrilling Rose Bowl game ever played—and no one ever again sneered at southern football."

Later versions of the Crimson Tide would also find their way to California, winning three more Rose Bowls, tying another, and losing only one. Players like Don Hutson, Millard "Dixie" Howell, and Harry Gilmer would make history in the bowl now known as "the granddaddy of them all." The Rose Bowl was so integral to the first half-century of Alabama football that it found its way into the program's fight song, "Yea, Alabama," which includes the memorable line: "Remember the Rose Bowl, we'll win then."

The coaches of those teams, Wallace Wade and Frank Thomas, built Alabama into an elite program long before there was the glare of television lights, or the madness of social media. And as the years went by, Wade and Thomas would be followed into legend

Nick Saban and the Crimson Tide. (Photo by Pete Pajor/*The Crimson White*, courtesy of the UA Office of Student Media)

by Paul "Bear" Bryant, who had contributed as a Bama player in one of those Rose Bowl victories and would become whom many consider the greatest coach of all time. That is, until Saban arrived in Tuscaloosa and began winning so much that even Crimson Tide faithful who were around in Bryant's years and adored him have begun to openly discuss if the unthinkable has happened. Has someone finally matched Bryant in the rarefied air at the top of college football history?

For all its championships, Alabama had fallen on hard times before Bryant came back to coach his alma mater in 1958. Instead of inheriting one of those storied Rose Bowl teams, Bryant faced the challenging task of rebuilding a program that had gone 4–24–2 in its last three years under coach J. B. "Ears" Whitworth, including a 17-game losing streak highlighted (or perhaps "lowlighted" would be a more accurate word) by the most disastrous year in Alabama football history—an 0–10 season in 1955. Bart Starr was a senior quarterback on that team but saw only sporadic playing time, thanks to nagging injuries and the coach's ill-fated decision to start underclassmen. Starr would go on to become a Hall of Fame NFL quarterback, leading the Green Bay Packers to victories in the first two Super Bowls—and winning the Most Valuable Player award in each of them.

The uphill job of rebuilding a once-proud program was not too big for Bryant. He led Alabama to a winning season in that first year, 1958, and by his fourth season, the Crimson Tide was back on top, winning a consensus national championship with an 11–0 run in 1961. It was a team with such a ferocious defense that it gave up just 25 points all season. The program that had once won Rose Bowls before losing its way in the 1950s was again the toast of college football. President John F. Kennedy was among the many dignitaries honoring Alabama players and their famous coach after the season.

Bryant's early star players at Alabama, including Lee Roy Jordan, Pat Trammell, and Billy Neighbors, would be followed by the likes of Joe Namath, Ray Perkins, Dennis Homan, Paul Crane, Ken Stabler, John Hannah, Johnny Musso, John Mitchell, Wilbur Jackson, and a litany of other players who survived and thrived under the coach's harsh, hard-driving practices and unforgiving expectations. All told, Bryant would break the record books, winning six national championships and 13 Southeastern Conference titles at Alabama and becoming, before he retired, the winningest college football coach ever.

His last championship came in 1979, and he died suddenly of a heart attack on January 26, 1983, just weeks after he announced his retirement. His death was a gut-wrenching blow to Alabama fans and seemed to cast a dark cloud over the program throughout much of the next decade. Bryant was, as the cliché goes, "a hard act to follow." Still, there were glimpses of greatness in Alabama teams during those years, including performances by some of the best defensive players in the game. Among them were linebackers Cornelius Bennett, whose thundering sack of Notre Dame quarterback Steve Beuerlein in a 1986 game remains legendary, and Derrick Thomas, who set an NCAA single-season record of 27 sacks in 1988, went on to an outstanding NFL career, and then died far too young.

There were other defining moments for Alabama in the 1980s, including a thrilling walk-off 52-yard field goal from kicker Van Tiffin to win the 1985 Iron Bowl game against Auburn at Birmingham's Legion Field. It became known simply as "The Kick."

But it took head coach Gene Stallings, who had played for Bryant's hardscrabble teams back at Texas A&M in the mid-1950s, to lead Alabama to another national championship. Stallings's undefeated 1992 Crimson Tide team, led by perhaps the best defense Alabama had fielded since 1961, won the inaugural SEC postseason championship game over Florida and weeks later routed the undefeated, highly favored Miami Hurricanes in the 1993 Sugar Bowl.

Alabama was back, at least for a time, though NCAA sanctions, inconsistent play, and a revolving door of coaches over the next 15 years would hinder the program's efforts at trying to win another national title. But the program would continue to produce plenty of memorable moments before Saban's arrival in 2007. The 1999 team, for instance, won the SEC championship in a 34–7 rout of Florida and showcased the best running back in the nation, Shaun Alexander, who would go on to win the NFL's Most Valuable Player award in 2005 with the Seattle Seahawks.

Nothing short of Bryant's era, however, could truly prepare the college football world for the dynasty that would begin not long after Saban took over as head coach in 2007. Having already won a national championship at LSU before a two-year stint as coach of the NFL's Miami Dolphins, Saban began installing what he called "the process" in Tuscaloosa. He demanded accountability from his players and assistant coaches and even chided fans to stay in their seats for the entirety of home games. In Saban's process, the fans had a role, too. "Do your job" was his mantra to everyone in the program. He also hit the recruiting trail, signing a series of classes that have been considered the best in college football.

In just Saban's third season at Alabama, the Crimson Tide won the 2009 national championship, defeating Texas 37–21 in the Bowl Championship Series title game. The victory was even more memorable because of the setting—Rose Bowl Stadium, where the Crimson Tide had first carved its name among the elite teams in history way back in 1926.

"This is not the end. This is the beginning," Saban said afterward. And he could not have been more accurate.

Alabama also won the 2011 BCS national title, defeating LSU 21–0 in the 2012 championship game in New Orleans, then came back the next season and defeated Georgia in a thriller for the SEC crown and afterward destroyed Notre Dame 42–14 in the 2013 BCS national championship game.

Still, the dynasty was far from over.

College football finally had a playoff, beginning with the 2014 season. Alabama was one of the four teams selected, and though the Tide lost to Ohio State in the semifinal held in the Sugar Bowl, it was back the following year. This time, Alabama would finish what it had started, winning the 2015 SEC championship game against Missouri, blowing out Michigan State 38–0 in the CFB playoff semifinal, and, in one of the most spectacular national championship games ever, defeated Clemson 45–40 at University of Phoenix Stadium in Glendale, Arizona.

Both Clemson and Alabama found themselves right back in the championship game a year later, and this time, Clemson scored on the game's last play from scrimmage to win a heartbreaker 35–31 over the Tide.

History, however, was not done with these two teams. They would meet again, for the third time in three years. The setting was a 2018 CFP semifinal in New Orleans, and Alabama won it going away, 24–6, to advance to the championship game against Georgia. For a while it looked like the Bulldogs would win their first national championship since 1980. They led Alabama 13–0 at halftime, before Saban made the gutsy decision to replace the Tide's two-year starting quarterback Jalen Hurts with freshman Tua Tagovailoa. It turned out to be a brilliant move. Led by Tagovailoa, Alabama rallied and had a chance to win it in regulation, only to have a 36-yard field goal sail wide to the left. That only made the ending in overtime even more dramatic. Tagovailoa's 41-yard touchdown pass to win it came on a second down and a country mile to go for a first down. (Actually, it was second and 26, which is enough.) The stunning finish sent shock waves throughout the stadium and across the nation. This book is about memorable moments, and it simply doesn't get any more memorable than that.

The victory gave Alabama its fifth national title in nine years and added yet another turbo boost to a dynasty that shows no signs of slowing down. It also gave Saban his sixth national championship, tying Bryant for the most ever. In his eleven seasons at Alabama, Saban now has a 132–20 record (winning an astonishing 86.8 percent of his games), and there is little doubt that as long as he continues to coach, championships will follow.

The list of players who have contributed at Alabama since Saban's arrival not only includes some of the best in college football, but many are also having an impact in the NFL. There are far too many to name here, but among them are: Julio Jones, Mark Ingram (the Tide's first Heisman Trophy winner), Mark Barron, Dont'a Hightower, Courtney Upshaw, Marcell Dareus, Amari Cooper, Landon Collins, Ha Ha Clinton-Dix, Derrick Henry (Alabama's second Heisman Trophy winner), Eddie Lacy, O. J. Howard, Marlon Humphrey, T. J. Yeldon, Arie Kouandjio, Reggie Ragland, C. J. Mosley, Eddie Jackson, A'Shawn Robinson, Kenyan Drake, and AJ McCarron.

Joining them will be a program-record 12 Crimson Tide players selected in the 2018 NFL Draft, including Minkah Fitzpatrick, Da'Ron Payne, Calvin Ridley, Rashaan Evans, Ronnie Harrison, Da'Shawn Hand, Anthony Averett, JK Scott, Shaun Dion Hamilton, Bradley Bozeman, Bo Scarbrough, and Joshua Frazier. All told, Alabama has had 77 players drafted over the past ten years, more than any other college football team.

The question in Tuscaloosa isn't whether the latest group of departing stars can be replaced. After all, freshmen like Tagovailoa, Smith, Jerry Jeudy, and Najee Harris played significant roles in the national championship game, and they will be there as Saban begins his twelfth season in Tuscaloosa. The real question is who will replace Saban when he decides to step down? For now, though, the dynasty rolls on.

PART ONE

THE THIN RED LINE BECOMES
THE CRIMSON TIDE

1

Birth of a College Football Powerhouse

It began quietly enough on a November 1892 afternoon in Lakeview Park, a sprawling, resort-like recreation area landscaped into the lower slope of Red Mountain on the southeast side of Birmingham, Alabama.

Four years earlier, in 1888, President Grover Cleveland had briefly visited this same site, stopping by the well-appointed Lakeview Hotel, which offered a rarity—running water in each of its guest rooms, and something far more rare: electric lights.

The hotel, which had since become a women's seminary, was located on a hill overlooking the park's signature man-made lake and within sight of two "dummy line" street rail tracks that could ferry parkgoers back and forth with ease. And visitors took full advantage, especially during the summer months, when they could enjoy any number of amenities, from concerts and performances at a covered outdoor stage to Lakeview's pavilion, which offered a bowling alley, roller skating, a dance floor, and beneath it in the basement, a swimming pool.

A year after Cleveland's visit, the man who defeated him for the presidency, Benjamin Harrison, also paid a quick visit while in town to give a speech on April 16, 1891. Harrison "was taken to Lakeview on a sightseeing tour on the dummy," so reported a prominent local bank's newsletter. "A man was sent ahead of the train on horseback to see that the tracks were clear for the chief executive. At the park the President was greeted by many prominent citizens of Birmingham."

If the possibilities seemed endless as America entered the nineteenth century's final decade, the feeling was even more optimistic in Birmingham, which was rapidly making the transition from a series of rural communities to an urban center. Only twenty years earlier, Birmingham had not even existed. It was founded in 1871 by the Elyton Land Company, the same group of railroad investors and businessmen who later developed Lakeview Park, a recreational oasis in a blue-collar town.

Since then, Birmingham's population had skyrocketed, from 800 in 1871 to an almost unbelievable 45,000-plus by 1891. It would double that in another decade, as mining and steel companies took advantage of deep iron ore and coal deposits in the hills and valleys throughout the area—and the railroad lines that provided transportation.

So by the time a team of oddly dressed young men with the big crimson-colored letters "UA" emblazoned on their white shirts and sweaters arrived at Lakeview Park on the afternoon of November 11, 1892, Birmingham had become known as the "Magic City" because of its remarkable growth.

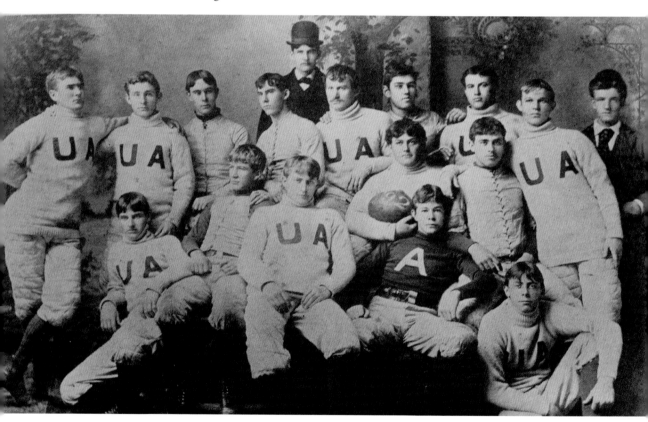

Alabama's first football team in 1892. William "Bill" Little is holding the football. Coach Eugene B. Beaumont Jr., in suit and derby hat, stands in the back. (From the 1931 edition of the *Corolla* yearbook, courtesy of the UA Office of Student Media)

But the magic was just beginning for this first-ever "foot ball" team from the state's flagship university fifty-five miles to the southwest in Tuscaloosa. The University of Alabama "Varsity" or "Cadets," as they were at first called because of the school's military history, could not have known the full implications of what they were starting as they prepared to play on Lakeview's baseball field—another of the park's wonders.

More than a century later, 100,000-plus people and a national television audience of millions would routinely watch Alabama play its football games in a soaring stadium back in Tuscaloosa that was lined with skyboxes, giant jumbo screens, and unimaginable pageantry. The team—now long since known as the Alabama Crimson Tide—would become the most elite college football program in the United States, winning five national championships in a nine-year span in the still-new twenty-first century, to go with multiple national titles won in six of the ten decades of the twentieth century.

It would likewise become a financial powerhouse, contributing the lion's share of $174 million that The University of Alabama athletics department reported in revenues for 2017 alone. Beyond that, the program has also had a major impact on national recruiting of not just athletes but nonathletes, as well. More than half of the 38,000 students attending UA in the 2017–18 school year were from out of state, and though they rank among the most academically accomplished students in the university's history, it's also a fair bet that the success of the football program most certainly made a favorable impression during their recruitment.

But for Alabama's inaugural college football team, there would be no live television broadcast, no streaming online coverage, no social media with its instant news, no radio, no giant stadium, and no fanfare to speak of as the players walked onto Lakeview Park's baseball field on November 11, 1892. They had left behind a campus back in Tuscaloosa with just 164 students, though a few made the trip with them.

The First Game

If ever there was a more inexperienced club in the still-new game of college football, it would have been hard to find. Only a couple of the eighteen Alabama cadets had ever played—or possibly even seen—a football game: one of them was William G. "Bill" Little, who would earn legendary status as the father of Alabama football.

Little, a University of Alabama law student, had taken up the game as a player while attending Phillips Academy, which was then, as now, regarded as one of the nation's most elite preparatory schools, in Andover, Massachusetts. A native of Livingston, Alabama—sixty miles southwest of Tuscaloosa—Little brought northeastern football with him when he returned home. It didn't take him long to interest his fellow UA students in this new game.

"Can you just imagine trying to teach somebody a new sport, a new game?" said Ken Gaddy, director of the Paul W. Bryant Museum at UA. "There was no high school feeder system like there is today, so you're walking onto a field to play for maybe the first time. When you show up to play, that's the first game you've ever seen."

Nevertheless, Bill Little did have some sense of what he was creating, predicting "Football is the game of the future in college life." As the cliché goes, truer words may have never been spoken. Though even Little could not have imagined the heights to which the game has now ascended, he would live long enough to see it become a wildly popular and successful sport at his alma mater. Three decades after the first game, Little would be there in 1926 to greet Crimson Tide players during a stopover at the Livingston train station as they returned home from an earth-shattering New Year's Day Rose Bowl victory over Washington in Los Angeles. The 20–19 win over the Huskies not only signaled the arrival of Alabama as a national college football power, it gave instant credibility to southern football, which had more or less continued to lag in reputation behind northern, midwestern, and western programs.

As for Little: "He got to enjoy the fruits of his labor, you might say, and to see that it had become a big-time sport," Gaddy said. "He was here when things really got going."

But there was no such fanfare and few spectators when Little and his fellow players finally lined up at Lakeview Park for their first game against a collection of high school players from Birmingham on that November Friday in 1892. It was considered something of an exhibition scrimmage at the time, as preparation for a game against an older and far more organized team from the Birmingham Athletic Club the next day. But the game would nevertheless go into the history books as UA's first contest, and first victory, a 56–0 win against the prep schoolers, or "Birmingham High School," as Alabama's football media guide now refers to them.

Scoring was much different in these still-beginning days of collegiate football. A field goal (at 5 points) was worth more than a touchdown (4 points). Points after tries counted 2 points and a safety counted 2 points, as it does now. No matter the scoring system, UA's team did a lot of it on that first day, scoring 28 points in each half in a game that looked more like a rugby match than what became modern football.

Legacies and Future Leaders

Though Little, as captain, was the leader of Alabama's team, he and his fellow students chose Eugene B. Beaumont Jr. as their coach. Beaumont just months earlier had been editor-in-chief of *The Pennsylvanian*, the student newspaper at the University of Pennsylvania in Philadelphia. Ironically, he was also the son of a Union officer who had led an attack against Confederate fortifications during the Battle of Selma, Alabama, on April 2, 1865. The elder Eugene B. Beaumont Sr. was awarded the Medal of Honor for his valor at both

Selma and an earlier battle in Tennessee. He was not among the detachment of Union soldiers who burned most of the buildings on the campus at The University of Alabama on April 22, 1865, just 20 days after the Selma battle and five days before Confederate Gen. Robert E. Lee surrendered his army at Appomattox Court House, Virginia, essentially ending the Civil War.

Beaumont Jr. participated in class football games, but not the varsity, at Penn, and covered the sport as a young journalist. According to later statements by at least two players on Alabama's 1892 team, had been recommended by Walter Camp, the famous Yale player, coach, and sportswriter whom many still consider the father of American football. The roster that Little and Beaumont had to work with was far from a simple ragtag team of students. They included two future leaders of the state and nation—halfback William B. Bankhead, who would later become speaker of the US House of Representatives and the father of famed actress Tallulah Bankhead, and substitute player Bibb Graves, who went on to serve two terms as Alabama's governor.

Eli Abbott, a 6-foot, 165-pound tackle, was considered to be the best player on the team and would become the club's coach, succeeding Beaumont a year later. Only Abbott and center H. M. Pratt stood 6 feet tall or better on the team. Although Little, a guard at 220 pounds, was an exception, the team was light in weight overall for a football club—averaging just 155 pounds. Soon enough, as subsequent Alabama teams would also be significantly outweighed by opponents yet continue to be competitive, sportswriters began calling them the "Thin Red Line." For now, however, there was the matter of a second game to play on less than a day's rest.

A 65-Yard Field Goal and a Stage Set for the First Iron Bowl

On November 12, 1892, the players met their match at Lakeview Park against the more experienced Birmingham Athletic Club. Alabama lost that game 5–4 on the strength of a stunning 65-yard drop-kick field goal by the Birmingham club's fullback, J. P. Ross.

"Over our heads went that ball as straight as a beggar can spit, over the goal," wrote Alabama players Burr Ferguson and Billy Walker, reminiscing decades later in a 1931 column for *The Crimson White*, the student newspaper. "We had no kicks, for we had seen a remarkable drop kick, and had had a wonderful time for 87 minutes and it took miracle stuff to beat us."

No one knows for sure if Ross broke a collegiate record that day, because records were spotty at best, but it served as a reminder that in the days when kicks were worth more points than touchdowns, good field-goal kickers might have been even more important than they are now. The good news for the Alabama club was that two weeks later these same two teams met yet again, and the cadets from Tuscaloosa took a 14–0 victory.

But ever since Bill Little returned to Alabama from Massachusetts and began talking about assembling a football team, there had been talk on campus about scheduling a game with the new team from across the state, Auburn. Both schools agreed to meet for the first time on February 22, 1893, at Lakeview Park. For Alabama, it would be considered the last game of their 1892 season. Auburn chose to count it as the first game of their 1893 season. But no matter the record keeping, one thing was certain: the game drew immediate interest from across the state. In sharp contrast to the sparse crowds who witnessed Alabama's first three games of the season, as many as 5,000 spectators would surround the baseball field at Lakeview to watch this one. It would become the first meeting between Alabama and Auburn in what is now one of college football's most storied rivalries—the Iron Bowl. And, like so many in subsequent years, it would be one to remember.

2

"It Was a Glorious Struggle": Forging the Iron Bowl

The 1890s were never as joyous or as prosperous for rank-and-file Americans as the term "Gay Nineties"—coined during a nostalgia craze decades later—made them out to be. To be sure, there was plenty to celebrate: Giant steam-powered passenger ships now routinely crisscrossed the oceans, opening up international travel to millions. Audiences watched the first demonstrations of motion pictures. Electricity slowly began to replace gas lighting, and chain-driven bicycles became all the craze.

But it was also a decade in which labor unrest was rampant. The lack of proper safety regulations led to many deaths in the workplace—including a series of mining fatalities in and around Birmingham—and the nation would slip into a major economic depression in 1893, brought about by a number of factors that included unbridled speculation on railroads.

Ironically, it had been the completion of north and south railroad lines at Jones Valley, site of what would become Birmingham, that led to the city's creation in 1871. The railroads were essential to hauling out the rich deposits of iron ore, coal, and limestone that made the city a near-perfect spot for iron and steel production. If the term "Magic City" seemed a bit over the top, another phrase began gaining popularity: "Pittsburgh of the South."

Later, Birmingham would lay claim to another title, "Football Capital of the South," which boosters emblazoned in big, bold letters across the upper deck of a stadium that first opened in 1927. And though that was well into the future, the city was about to be treated to an exciting preview of what lay ahead.

Rivals

By now, midway through December 1892, Alabama's inaugural football team was no longer a band of greenhorns. They had played three games, won two of them, and gained valuable experience. All along, however, they and a growing number of fans who followed their exploits in the newspapers had been keenly aware that they were not the only college football team in the state.

In fact, there was a group of young men at the Agriculture and Mechanical College of Alabama—located in Auburn, 150 miles southeast of Tuscaloosa—who had become the first in the state to play an intercollegiate football game earlier that same year. Auburn, as the team was called (even before the school officially changed the name to Auburn University), traveled to Atlanta and defeated a team from The University of Georgia on February 20, 1892.

After a layoff of nearly nine months, Auburn played three more games in Atlanta and by the end of November had a 2–2 record and, perhaps more important, a rival over in Tuscaloosa who was keeping score.

One hundred and twenty-five years later, as the Alabama Crimson Tide dominated American modern college football in the second decade of the twenty-first century, it became a running joke for fans of other programs to display "We Want Bama" signs throughout stadiums across the country. But in the late fall of 1892, it was a different story: for Alabama, at least, Auburn was the team to beat.

"We want to play Auburn a game of foot ball and we want to play them bad," editors of the *Journal*, a monthly student publication at UA, wrote in the November 1892 issue. "The correspondent of the Montgomery Advertiser, of recent date, from Auburn, seems to wish to create the impression that we are afraid of them, when Mr. (George) Petrie, their manager, knows and will tell anybody that asks him that we have written time and time again for a date in Montgomery on the 10th of December. Auburn, if we meet you, and are beaten, we will take it like men; but don't send out incorrect reports through newspapers: they might mislead the public."

But a December 10 date with Auburn was not to be: that was the date Alabama instead defeated the Birmingham Athletic Club 14–0 and ended the calendar year with a 2–1 record. But there was one more game to play before the Cadets from Tuscaloosa considered the season over. After some back-and-forth negotiating, the team got its wish: Alabama and Auburn agreed to play each other for the first time on February 22, 1893, at Lakeview Park, in the shadow of the hills where iron ore was being mined south of Birmingham. If ever there was an appropriate name for what would become a monumental rivalry in college football, the "Iron Bowl" was most certainly it, though nobody would actually call it that for years to come.

The Game

They began arriving in droves after journeys from both universities and from all corners of the state. Most used the rail lines, with extra cars added to meet the soaring demand, while others arrived on horseback, still others in carriages, and a good many on foot. Lakeview Park had seen its share of crowds on summer weekends, but no one had ever seen anything quite like this. The one ticket booth was far too inadequate to handle the demand. Organizers began walking through the crowd gathered outside the baseball field, selling tickets for 25 cents each.

The Daily News, which two years later would be renamed *The Birmingham News*, put it this way: "The vast surging throng kept its temper and the women took being jostled around good naturedly. As soon as the crowd got on the inside, the men unaccompanied by ladies made a rush for both sides of the grounds and soon were a dozen deep around the ropes, which were put up around the grid-iron. The east side of the field had been set apart for those in carriages, and soon from one end to the other it was filled with vehicles of all descriptions, gaily decorated in blue and gold, and in white and red. Both the grand stands were literally packed with people, making a most artistic picture as the colors of the schools in conjunction with women blended most artistically."

A fourth area, the bleachers, "were filled with as jolly a lot of men as ever sat on hard planks, and from their faces and their merry talk it was evident they had come out to make a happy afternoon of it," *The Daily News* reported.

Five Birmingham police officers were there to maintain order, but they were powerless to keep many in the crowd from surging past the ropes and onto the field to be closer to the action. As Alabama's 18 players, their head coach, and two assistants entered the field shortly before 3 p.m., they were met with thunderous cheers.

"Every man, woman and child who wore the red and white rose and shouted themselves hoarse," wrote *The Daily News*. The Cadets wore their by-now-familiar white uniforms accented with red stockings and large red letters "UA" on their sweaters.

Minutes later, Auburn arrived to wild cheers from their own fans. Their players were each dressed in a blue sweater with a large orange "A" on the front, and blue-and-white leg stockings.

Both teams immediately began warming up, alternating between kicking, tackling, and catching the ball. *The Daily News'* coverage read almost like a romance novel, noting that their "handsome" faces, "broad shoulders, strong lithe limbs, and powerful arms were the admiration of the young and old of each sex."

By 3:30 p.m., the game was ready to begin. Alabama was led by its captain, Bill Little, the man who had created this team and played left guard. The other ten starters included quarterback W. M. "Billy" Walker, fullback William "Will" Bankhead, halfbacks G. H. "Hub" Kyser and Dan Smith, right end D. A. Grayson, left end Burr Ferguson, right guard Robert E. Lee Cope—who played the entire game with his right hand in a plaster cast—left tackle Eli Abbott, right tackle F. M. "Pop" Savage, and center H. M. Pratt.

Auburn got the ball first, and quarterback J. C. Dunham immediately gained 10 yards on a flying wedge, by then one of the most popular plays in college football, in which players lined up in a V-formation and charged forward with the ball carrier in the middle. The play set the tone for a game that would be characterized by explosive runs, including at least 11 rushes for 20 yards or more. Two runs—both from Auburn—went for 65-yard touchdowns, including one from Tom Daniels in the first half and a crucial fumble scoop and score touchdown by halfback R. T. Dorsey just after the start of the second half. Auburn led 14–12 at half-time, but Dorsey's long touchdown return of an Alabama fumble broke open the game. Auburn widened its lead to 32–18 before Alabama added a late touchdown. The final score was 32–22, giving Auburn bragging rights in the first-ever meeting between the two schools.

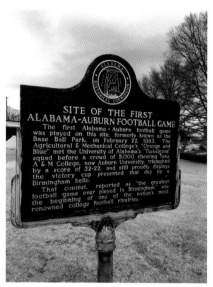

Historical marker in Birmingham commemorating the first Iron Bowl. (Photo by Mark Mayfield)

The next day, in a page-one recap that *The Daily News* headlined "Auburn Won! It was a glorious struggle," the newspaper praised both teams and noted there had been only one punt, by Alabama, in the entire game.

"A marked feature of the game was almost a total lack of punting on each side. The game was an offensive one, neither side cared to be on the defensive. This was shown by a few times which the ball was lost by either team on 4 downs."

Though Alabama had lost, it had proven its mettle against a good opponent, with plenty of success running the football. One highlight was a 30-yard touchdown sweep around Auburn's left end by Bill Little, the Tuscaloosa Cadets' captain and founder. It would be Little's last game. His team finished its first season with a 2–2 record.

Immediately after the game, a trophy cup was presented to Auburn's team on behalf of the city of Birmingham. "Drink from it and remember the victory you have won this day," the presenter, Delma Wilson, told Auburn captain Tom Daniels. "May you and your team live to see many more victories."

And then, as *The Daily News* noted, "A series of cheers rent the air and then the sun went down, blotting out the day on which the greatest foot ball game was ever played in Alabama."

3

They Call Alabama the Crimson Tide

No matter the loss to Auburn, the Cadets from Tuscaloosa had established what would eventually become a monumentally successful football program. The first season's record, at 2–2, was nothing to be ashamed of, especially when Alabama had outscored its opponents 96–37, though that included the 56–0 blowout win over Birmingham High School. But against solid competition in two games with the Birmingham Athletic Club and one with Auburn, the Cadets had still outscored their opponents 40 to 37 overall.

Nevertheless, there would be a coaching change. Eugene B. Beaumont, the former University of Pennsylvania student newspaper editor and son of a Union Civil War hero, was replaced by Eli Abbott, a tackle on the 1892 team and now a player-coach. The university's yearbook, *Corolla*, made no attempt to sugarcoat the coaching change: "We were unfortunate in securing a coach. After keeping him for a short time, we found that his knowledge of the game was very limited. We, therefore, 'got rid of' him, and under the excellent training of our much loved captain, we were placed in good condition by the time Mr. Abbott arrived to coach us."

Abbott, a native of Mississippi, had a connection to the University of Pennsylvania, like Beaumont. Abbott was even listed as a substitute on Penn's 1893 and 1894 teams, even as he played and coached at Alabama, presumably showing up periodically to help out in Philadelphia, given that Alabama's schedule was just four games each season in 1893 and '94 and Penn played a whopping total of 27 games over those two years. Penn had long established itself as a northern football power, and the school's 1894 team finished the season with a 12–0 record and was retroactively named national champions that year by at least one rating service.

No matter the coaching change at Alabama, the real problem was replacing at least

11

seven of the eleven starters from the '92 team. And it proved to be too much of a challenge. Abbott's 1893 team failed to win a game, going 0–4. Though his 1894 Alabama team rebounded to 3–1, including the team's first win over Auburn (an 18–0 victory in a game played in Montgomery), Alabama fell back to 0–4 in 1895. Abbott gave up the coaching job afterward, reportedly going back to Penn to earn an undergraduate degree in 1896. He would return to UA in 1902 to coach the team for a single year.

Coaching changes were routine for Alabama in the early years of its football program: seven different men served as head coach for the Cadets in their first decade. Money to pay coaches was hard to come by, usually paid by students. Abbott's replacement as coach in 1896, Otto Wagonhurst, was also connected to Penn, having played football there on outstanding teams from 1892 through 1895.

He lasted just that one 1896 season in Tuscaloosa, leading the team to a 2–1 record, before moving on to the University of Iowa. In an anecdote that underscored the sort of controlled chaos that existed around Alabama's program at the time, Wagonhurst was paid just $250 of his promised $750 salary. Thirty years later, after Alabama won its first Rose Bowl game, the university's athletic association located Wagonhurst in Akron, Ohio, and sent him the remaining $500 that he was owed.

No matter the coaches, the first decade of Alabama football was marked by starts and stops, as concerns increasingly grew over violence in a hard-hitting sport where players participated without headgear and adequate protective padding. Some games looked more like brawls than athletic competition.

Thomas Wert, who played one year at Auburn before his selection as captain of Alabama's 1899 team, recalled the frenzy surrounding those early games.

"I had played under the famous J. W. Heisman, and in those days, football wasn't a lady's game," Wert told *The Crimson White* decades later. "When one of the Mississippi players tried to move the ball after it was dead, I fell on his neck with my knee. I hadn't done so before the entire grandstand was empty and the people came on me with umbrella, walking canes and the like and if it hadn't been for a bunch of policemen surrounding me, I'm afraid I would have been knocked out myself."

The following day, on November 25, 1899, Alabama traveled to New Orleans to take on the Southern Athletic Club, which Wert described as an assortment of "prizefighters" and "dockhands," among others.

"They kicked me, trampled me, and sometimes bit me, all at the same time," he said. "No prizefighter was ever beaten up worse than I was and the whole team was in the same fix."

Just a year earlier, in 1898, Alabama's still-new football program had been left for dead, with the school fielding no team at all that season. And the team had played just one game in 1897—a 6–0 victory over Tuscaloosa Athletic Club. The downturn came after university trustees banned the team from traveling, citing concerns about both academics and increasing violence in football. Students vehemently complained about the ban, citing the inability of the program to draw a large enough paying audience in Tuscaloosa, and the difficulty in scheduling games. Unlike today, with more than 38,000 students enrolled, just 200 students attended the university in the 1897–98 academic year.

"We have seen that it is useless to attempt to put out a football team so long as we are compelled to play all of our games on the campus," wrote editors of the 1899 *Corolla* yearbook.

An editor at *The Crimson White*, the student newspaper, also addressed the issue, writing, "The people of Tuskaloosa take so little interest in athletics at the University that they will not turn out for games. . . . If the trustees do not allow the teams to travel, it is my opinion that athletics are dead at the University of Alabama."

By the fall of 1899, the trustees relented, and Alabama would only miss two other seasons in its storied history—both due to world wars, in 1918 and in 1943. At the turn of the twentieth century, it was clear that Alabama was a program still trying to find its way. By 1904, however, when the team played a ten-game schedule for the first time, going 7–3 in the process, the program was beginning to make a name for itself—and regularly playing teams that would later become part of the Southeastern Conference: Auburn, Tennessee, LSU, Ole Miss, Mississippi State, Vanderbilt, and Georgia.

Alabama had won its share of games against most of these teams as it prepared to play Auburn for the twelfth time on November 16, 1907, at Birmingham's Fair Grounds, which had by now replaced Lakeview Park as the venue when the teams were not playing either in Montgomery or on UA's campus in Tuscaloosa. Auburn led the series 7–4, but Alabama had won the last two meetings, 30–0 and 10–0.

Overall, the "Thin Red Line" from Tuscaloosa had gone 18–8 in the three seasons

Train to the game in 1907. (From the *Corolla* yearbook, courtesy of the UA Office of Student Media)

leading up to 1907, its most successful run so far, and was 3–1–1 as it met Auburn in what no one could have known would be the last time these two teams would play for 41 years. Already tension between the two teams had been rising. A year earlier, in advance of the 1906 game, Auburn had formally protested the participation of Alabama player T. C. Sims, claiming he was ineligible because he had taken time off from school and, though he had returned, had not registered early enough to play. Alabama coach J. H. "Doc" Pollard countered, saying Sims had registered within the necessary 30 days before the seasons started. The Southern Inter-Collegiate Athletic Association, to which both Alabama and Auburn belonged, ruled in Alabama's favor. It was far from the only claim of ineligible players levied by the two schools over the previous eleven contests. Pollard, who would go on to become Alabama football's first 20-game winner as a coach (with a 21–4–5 record over four seasons), was fond of using shifts and less common formations to create an edge for his team. Pollard had reportedly installed one of them, the "military formation," in secret practices in Tuscaloosa. It called for the entire line, except the center, to step back

At the 1907 Alabama-Auburn game. (From the *Corolla*, courtesy of the UA Office of Student Media)

behind the line of scrimmage, join hands, and before the ball was snapped rush back up to the line, often on the opposite side from which they had originally been set. The effect was an unbalanced line.

"The ball would then be snapped and the play set in motion. This play produced gain after gain," wrote author James Edson in the 1946 book *Alabama's Crimson Tide*.

Another big crowd of 5,000 or more was on hand as Alabama and Auburn met in the rain at the Birmingham Fair Grounds. Auburn, with a 6–1 record, was a heavy favorite, despite having lost two consecutive games to Alabama, in 1905 and 1906. Though the "Crimson Whites," as some were now calling them, had come in to the game with a respectable 3–1–1 record, the one loss had been a 54–4 rout by Sewanee. Auburn had also lost to Sewanee, but only by a 12–6 margin.

Touchdowns, now five points each, finally counted more than field goals, which for another couple of years would still be worth four points. It turned out to be a defensive battle, with each team managing only a touchdown and extra point, ending in a 6–6 tie on a muddy field. The Thin Red Line could have won it outright had Alabama team captain Emile Hannon not missed a 15-yard field goal "directly in front of the goal posts," as James Edson later described it in his book.

Nevertheless, a tie was deemed almost as good as a victory for Alabama, considering sportswriters had listed them as 3–1 underdogs. It would be the only tie ever recorded in the Iron Bowl series. And more important, the game gave Alabama its now-iconic nickname.

Hugh Roberts, sports editor of *The Birmingham Age-Herald*, alluding to Alabama players giving it their all in uniforms smeared with red mud, referred to them as a "Crimson Tide." Years later, another Birmingham sports writer, Henry "Zipp" Newman, regularly used the nickname in his coverage, increasing its popularity to the point that mentions of the Thin Red Line eventually disappeared from newspaper coverage, replaced by the Crimson Tide.

While the 1907 game produced a new nickname, it is also known for something else: due to what, in hindsight, appear to be petty squabbles over a few dollars of player per diem travel allotment, choice of officials, the number of players on travel teams, and scheduling conflicts, it would be the last time the two rivals would meet for the next 41 years. They renewed the series in 1948 following threats from the Alabama Legislature to withhold funding from both universities if they did not voluntarily agree to meet on the football field again. But that was well into the future. For now, Alabama would have to build its program without a game against its cross-state rival. It would manage just fine.

4

George H. Denny and the Beginning of "Built by Bama"

Denny Chimes rises 115 feet above the sprawling quad at The University of Alabama. The bell tower has become an iconic symbol of the university and is one of the most photographed structures not only on campus, but in the entire state. Completed in 1929, it is dedicated to a man who transformed UA from a small, sleepy state school of 400 students (and just 55 of them women) when he became the school's president in 1912 to nearly 5,000 students, many from out of state and more than 1,000 of them women, over the next two decades.

Yet, it wasn't simply the number of students that skyrocketed under the leadership of George H. "Mike" Denny. The campus more than doubled in size during his tenure, adding 23 academic buildings—many of them funded with private money—along with a sharp rise in the number of faculty members. The growth included a flurry of new centers for study, among them the College of Commerce and Business Administration (now the Culverhouse College of Commerce), the College of Education, and the College of Home Economics (now the College of Human Environmental Sciences), along with premed studies, engineering courses, and departments of music and art that greatly expanded the Arts & Sciences program. Denny also created extension centers throughout Alabama that helped lead to the creation of at least three other state universities, including the University of Alabama at Birmingham, the University of South Alabama in Mobile, and the University of Alabama in Huntsville.

Nowhere, however, was Mike Denny's imprint more noticeable than in the football program in Tuscaloosa, which he helped to expand and enjoyed immensely during his 25 years as UA president (and again during a one-year interim term in 1941–42). He was often at practices and more than once got so close to the action that he was knocked

Denny Chimes at The University of Alabama.
(Photo by Mark Mayfield)

down by players making tackles. It was said that whenever Denny took a fall at practice, the team was sure to have a winning season. By that reckoning, he may have been on his back more often than not at practice, because Alabama did plenty of winning during his tenure as president.

The program had established a decent but not spectacular record of 65–42–9 before Denny arrived on campus in 1912 after serving as president of Virginia's Washington and Lee University. During the next 25 years with Denny as UA president, the Crimson Tide's record would be among the best in the nation at 171–45–11 and included three national championships and three Rose Bowl victories.

Students, alumni, and faculty so admired Denny that they privately raised the $100,000 necessary in 1928 for the construction of the bell tower to honor him. Denny Chimes was dedicated in 1929, the same year a new 12,000-seat football stadium, also named for him, was completed. Today Bryant-Denny Stadium seats nearly 102,000 fans, and there is no question that Mike Denny would approve of what the university and the football program have become since his time.

A Victory for the Ages in Philadelphia

Alabama is now, of course, an elite program nationally, but it took Denny and a string of some outstanding coaches to first establish such a rich tradition. If there was one moment in Denny's early tenure that was a turning point, it had to be on a November afternoon in an otherwise ordinary season in 1922, when the Crimson Tide traveled north to Philadelphia to meet the undefeated University of Pennsylvania Quakers. Penn had been named national champions at least six times during the late nineteenth century and the first decade of the twentieth century and was well on its way to recapturing that glory, particularly after a victory over powerful Navy a week before the Alabama game. Coached by John

Scenes from 1922 Alabama football season. (From the *Corolla* yearbook, courtesy of the UA Office of Student Media)

Heisman, whose named would later be immortalized with the Heisman Trophy, Penn was an overwhelming favorite to defeat Alabama and move on to a much-anticipated in-state rival game with Pittsburgh.

Alabama, however, had other plans. The team from Tuscaloosa was coached by Xen-ophon "Xen" Scott, whom Denny had hired to bring the football program back in 1919 after the university had canceled the football season in 1918 due to World War I. Scott may have at first seemed an odd choice: he had been a sportswriter, covering horse racing in Cleveland, Ohio. But he also had plenty of football credentials, having played and coached at Western Reserve University in Cleveland and later served as head coach at Case School of Applied Science (the schools are now merged as Case Western Reserve University). Scott also had experience as an assistant coach at Penn State.

Denny's instincts in choosing him had been right: Scott would become Alabama's sec-ond 20-game winner, with a record of 29–9–3 over four seasons, including an 8–1 record in that first year of 1919 and a 10–1 record (Alabama's first ten-win season) in 1920. But none of those accomplishments could match what Scott and his team did on November 4, 1922, when more than 22,000 fans showed up at Penn's newly renovated Franklin Field to watch what most thought would be a breather against the men from Tuscaloosa.

Unknown to those outside the program, Scott was battling cancer during the entire 1922 season and had already turned in his resignation to Denny weeks before the Penn game. Nevertheless, he had prepared his team well, despite visible signs of weight loss. The Alabama team that stepped on the field was more than a match for the mighty Quakers. By now, touchdowns in college football counted six points and field goals three. Alabama scored first early in the second quarter with a 35-yard field goal from kicker Bull Wesley, but Penn came right back with a 28-yard touchdown run from its star, George Sullivan. A successful extra point try gave Penn a 7–3 halftime lead.

But "from the start, it was evident that Alabama was unexpectedly strong," *The Philadelphia Inquirer* reported in its coverage the following day. "They proved to have a smash-ing line attack, worked from a triple tandem formation, with the quarter-back receiving the pass and turning the ball over to either the second or last man in the attacking trio. More, they have a fast and elusive warrior in (Charles) Bartlett to turn the wing—a triple threat, for this same heroic Southerner threw forward passes and matched (Penn's) Hamer in punting. Then, too, they had a dangerous field goal kicker in Wesley, and last, but by no means least, a stonewall line that stubbornly refused to either break or even bend very much."

It was Bartlett who, in the third quarter, took off on a 29-yard run, down to Penn's 6-yard line to set up a winning touchdown for Alabama. Three plays later, Alabama was in the end zone on a dive play by halfback Allen MacCartee, according to the *Inquirer's* coverage. Bull Wesley's extra point try sailed wide, but it didn't matter. Alabama had taken a 9–7 lead that it would never give up.

The victory made national news and was hailed as a defining moment for southern football. The stacked series of headlines above the game story in *The New York Times* said it all: "Alabama's Eleven Humbles Old Penn," "Southerners, Underestimated," "Gain Notable 9 to 7 Victory on Franklin Field," "QUAKERS CAUGHT NAPPING."

The beginning of *The Philadelphia Inquirer*'s main story on the game fully captured the significance, and shock, of Alabama's win.

"A Crimson Tide rolled out of the Sunny South yesterday to wash all the joy out of a Penn Football Renaissance, to flood the eyes of the Quakers with tears, and inundate the new stadium beneath a Niagara of grief, desolation and blasted hopes. It was the burly gridiron gladiators of the University of Alabama, a despised football army, which swept into Franklin Field from far off Tuscaloosa to drive the best team Penn has had in years back to the football wilderness— the gloomy land where roam the defeated. It was an unfeared eleven supposed only to furnish a prac-

tice game which smote the Red and Blue hip and thigh right at the moment when the Quaker heroes basked in the glory of a dazzling triumph over the Navy."

The Crimson Tide's victory set off wild celebrations back home, and a massive crowd greeted the team on their arrival at the Tuscaloosa train station. The team would go on to win three of its final four games, including blowout victories over LSU and Mississippi State, and finish the season with a 6–3–1 record. But nothing could come close to the euphoria over the victory in Philadelphia. It set the stage for even greater victories to soon come. Sadly, though, it would be Xen Scott's last year of coaching. He died in 1924 from the cancer that he valiantly fought while leading Alabama to prominence.

Dr. George "Mike" Denny looked to Nashville, Tennessee, for the next Alabama football coach, trying to hire Vanderbilt head coach Dan McGugin. But the Vandy coach recommended

President George Denny. (From the *Corolla*, courtesy of the UA Office of Student Media)

one of his assistant football coaches instead—Wallace Wade, who was also the school's head basketball and baseball coach. Wade had played football at Brown University and had participated in the 1916 Rose Bowl.

He took over Alabama's program beginning with the 1923 season, and in less three short years, he would return to the Rose Bowl, this time with the Crimson Tide. And neither Alabama nor college football would ever be the same again.

PART TWO

REMEMBER THE ROSE BOWL: ALABAMA GOES NATIONAL

A Hollywood Ending in Los Angeles

The talk among Alabama football players and coaches on a train ride back to Tuscaloosa following a 27–0 Thanksgiving Day rout of Georgia in Birmingham in 1925 focused on whether the Crimson Tide might be invited—for the first time ever—to play an extra game following a glorious undefeated season.

This was no idle discussion. At stake was the biggest prize of all: a chance to play in the Rose Bowl in Pasadena, California. Not only was it the most prestigious game in college football, it was the only postseason contest. And no southern team had yet been invited to participate in it.

Despite Alabama's landmark victory over Penn in 1922, Southern football had still not consistently risen to a level that adequately impressed the Tournament of Roses committee in California. Rose Bowl officials, according to an *Associated Press* report near the end of the 1925 season, seemed more interested in bringing another eastern power like undefeated Dartmouth or undefeated but twice-tied Colgate to the game to face the Pacific Coast Conference's juggernaut, 10–0–1 Washington, which despite the one tie had outscored its opponents by a whopping 461–39 margin.

But this 1925 Alabama team, the one making its way back on a "football special" train to Tuscaloosa, was hard to ignore. With the Georgia victory just a couple of hours earlier, Alabama had secured its second consecutive Southern Conference championship, and a perfect 9–0 record. Remarkably, eight of those nine wins had been shutouts. Only one team, nonconference foe Birmingham-Southern, had managed to score on Alabama, and the Crimson Tide had dispatched them by a 50–7 score. All told, Alabama outscored its opponents 277–7, including blowout wins over LSU, Kentucky, Florida, Sewanee, and

Georgia, along with closer margins, but shutouts nonetheless, over Mississippi State and Georgia Tech.

Not only had the Crimson Tide just finished the most spectacular regular season in its 33-year history, it was also a team with star power, including two future College Football Hall of Famers: hard-nosed, tough-running quarterback Allison "Pooley" Hubert and flashy halfback Johnny Mack Brown, who was among the fastest players in college football. He also had the kind of good looks and charisma that would eventually be noticed by filmmakers in Hollywood.

Alabama was led by head coach Wallace Wade, a former Vanderbilt assistant who had been hired beginning with the 1923 season and had—as the 1925 team finished the regular season—established an outstanding 24–3–1 record. At 33 years old, Wade remained one of the youngest head football coaches in the nation, and easily one of the sternest. Known for putting his players through long, grueling practice drills, Wade was a no-nonsense disciplinarian who had little patience for anyone on his team who wasn't

Johnny Mack Brown. (From the *Corolla*, courtesy of the UA Office of Student Media)

obsessed with perfection on every play. He was as intimidating to his own players as they were becoming to opponents on the field.

"When we went out for football at Alabama, we were expected to practice all afternoon," Johnny Mack Brown told *Sports Illustrated* decades later. "Wallace Wade always told us, 'A good football player never gets hurt.'"

For now, though, on that train ride back to Tuscaloosa, the talk turned to the $1,000 per game that Brown, a senior, had apparently been offered to immediately turn pro now that his final regular season was over. Already, two famous All-American college players in 1925—Red Grange at the University of Illinois and Ernie Nevers at Stanford University—had signed lucrative pro football contracts after their final college games several days earlier. Both would begin playing exhibition pro games immediately in December.

If he accepted, Brown, who had reportedly been promised $5,000 for five games—a substantial amount in 1925 but considerably less than what Nevers and Grange had been offered—would quickly join Nevers and other former college all-stars in Jacksonville, Florida, for a series of exhibition games against NFL teams.

But Alabama had an unprecedented chance to extend its season. No matter if the Rose Bowl was looking elsewhere or not—even to Alabama's fellow Southern Conference team, Tulane in New Orleans—an invitation was still a possibility for the Crimson Tide. And Wade and his players knew it. The problem for Brown was that his decision could not wait on the Rose Bowl. One thing was clear: signing a pro contract now would end Brown's college eligibility. Others on the Alabama team may also have also had similar offers. None accepted. Despite the temptation, the opportunity to play in the Rose Bowl outweighed a quick payoff. At least that's the way it turned out.

"This is the story of a young halfback of a few seasons ago who passed up a chance to make 5000 bucks by playing pro-football in order to be on deck if his alma mater landed a post-season football game they were dickering for," wrote Bob Matherne in a National Enterprise Association (NEA) news service story published three years later, after Brown had become a Hollywood actor. "The point is—[Brown] passed up the 5000 bucks, played in the post-season game, and landed in the movies."

But such a film script-like ending for Brown and his teammates had yet to play out on that Thanksgiving Day of 1925. It was soon set in motion, however, when Dartmouth and Colgate each reportedly declined the opportunity to make the long cross-country trip to Los Angeles over the holiday break. And though Tulane was considered as well and may have also nixed the Rose Bowl's inquiries, Alabama received the invitation, and the players quickly accepted. Afterward, Rose Bowl representative Jack Benefield, who served as athletic manager at the University of Oregon, denied that others had declined invitations.

"This is the first invitation that has been offered by anyone," Benefield said, according to an account in the 1977 book *Bowl Bama Bowl*. "I did take the matter up with Colgate authorities, but their request for time to consider was out of the question. Tulane, nor any other college, has not been authored an invitation as only feelers were sent out."

It no longer mattered whether Alabama had been a second, third, or even fourth choice. They were going to the Rose Bowl. The Washington Huskies, also called the "Purple Tornado" by sportswriters at the time, had at first reportedly rejected an invitation to the game but quickly changed their minds. The game was on. And Alabama was a huge underdog and getting little, if any, respect on the West Coast.

Even nationally known humorist Will Rogers got in on the act, calling Alabama "that team from Tusca-loser." Others took even worse shots, with one West Coast sportswriter, noting the huge size difference between the teams, predicting a 51-point Washington victory. Stanford's popular coach, Glenn "Pop" Warner, was far more kind but still noted of Alabama: "They've got speed, but they're too light to stop that big Washington team."

A 1962 story in *Sports Illustrated*, recapping the historic game 36 years earlier, described the prevailing notion among national sports analysts: "It was considered by many to be the worst mismatch in the history of the game. Alabama had a good enough record—nine straight wins—but football experts in the '20s all knew that southern football was barely on a level with junior varsity play in the rest of the country."

Said Johnny Mack Brown in a 1961 interview that was later included in an Alabama Public Television documentary, *Roses of Crimson*: "In those days Alabama or the southern teams weren't noted as having great football potential. It seems that they thought perhaps that we were lazy and full of hookworms or something of that sort, but nevertheless, after winning a couple of conference championships back in the south, we were invited out to play against the University of Washington, which at that time was one of the greatest football teams in America."

Like Brown, Washington's biggest star, a big running back named George "Wildcat" Wilson, had reportedly rejected a major offer to turn pro before the Rose Bowl game. Neither player would regret it, and each would have a huge impact on the game.

There was, of course, no social media or Internet, no cell phones, no ESPN, and no television of any sort. But the game dominated conversations throughout Alabama and across the South. Wrote editors in the December 1925 issue of *Rammer-Jammer*, an irreverent and well-respected student humor and literary magazine at UA: "In about a week, the football team goes to California to show the natives a few tricks. Everyone else goes home. Now, why in the name of all that is patriotic should we let a small matter of three thousand miles keep us from being with the Crimson Tide in their sortie. We can, in spirit, at least. Who knows but what there is something in this mental telepathy after all."

Twenty-two Alabama players and their coaches boarded a train in Tuscaloosa on

December 19 to begin the long ride to Los Angeles. They arrived in Pasadena on Christmas Eve after the five-day train ride that included frequent stops for meals, workouts, and a brief tour of the Grand Canyon. There were inordinate demands on the players' time once in California, particularly from University of Alabama alumni living in Los Angeles, who were thrilled their alma mater would now play on the biggest stage in college football. Along with practices, the Crimson Tide players visited movie studios and got to meet Hollywood film stars.

But the spotlight also fell on the players themselves: *Birmingham News* sports writer Henry "Zipp" Newman wrote: "Pooley Hubert and Johnny Mack Brown will have enough experience posing for the cameramen to enter the movies." In Brown's case, Newman proved to be prophetic. The Alabama halfback would get a film screen test in 1927 and go on to become one of the era's most successful stars of Hollywood westerns.

For now, though, the sideshow that was developing around Alabama's players greatly concerned their coach. Wallace Wade called a halt to the nonfootball activities on December 28. For the remainder of the visit, the team would be confined to their hotel—the Huntington—and Wade ordered practices to be closed to the public in preparation for the big game.

Washington's team, by contrast, didn't show up in Pasadena until a day before the game, preferring to prepare back on campus in Seattle.

The day of the game—January 1, 1926—turned tragic when a Tournament of Roses Parade viewing grandstand collapsed, killing eight people instantly, and three others later died from their injuries. Two other parade watchers also died in accidents unrelated to the grandstand collapse. It remains the deadliest day in Rose Bowl history.

Though the game paled in importance to the lives lost at what should have been a joyous day at the parade, it nevertheless went on as scheduled, drawing a capacity crowd of 45,000—the most people to ever see an Alabama game up until that time. Back home, Alabama movie theaters were jammed with crowds there to keep up with the game, with announcers reading play-by-play reports via telegram news tickers.

At the start, it seemed the pundits who predicted a Washington rout of Alabama were correct. The Crimson Tide fell behind 12–0 at halftime. It seemed they could not stop George Wilson, who barreled through the Alabama line and when he wasn't doing that intercepted an Alabama pass and even threw a touchdown pass. Wilson, however, left the game with an injury late in the second quarter, an ominous development for Washington, though he would return in the fourth quarter.

Throughout the first half, Alabama had not fully implemented its offense, preferring to keep quarterback Pooley Hubert's runs to a minimum early against the huge Washington defensive line. "I don't want you to run in the first half," Wallace Wade told Hubert

Alabama at the 1926 Rose Bowl. (From the *Corolla*, courtesy of the UA Office of Student Media)

on the train ride to California, according to the 1962 recap in *Sports Illustrated*. "Let's see how that Washington line shapes up. You know what happened to (Ernie) Nevers when he played against Washington." (Nevers was knocked out of that game, although he returned late in the contest.)

Wade was forced to make halftime adjustments: he instructed Hubert to run the ball more and moved guards Bruce Jones and Ben Enis to opposite ends on defense to stop Washington's perimeter runs. A reenergized Alabama team was more than ready for the second half.

Following a Washington punt that sailed out of bounds on its own 42-yard line, Hubert ran the ball five consecutive times, finally plunging into the end zone from the 1-yard line, scoring Alabama's first touchdown. The Crimson Tide's Bill Buckler successfully

Pooley Hubert. (From the *Corolla*, courtesy of the UA Office of Student Media)

Part Two

kicked an extra point (something Washington had failed to do after the Huskies' two first-half touchdowns), and Alabama trailed 12–7.

With Wilson sidelined with bruised ribs, Washington again failed to move the ball. For Alabama, it was prime time for Johnny Mack Brown. Speeding down the sideline, then cutting across the middle, he hauled in a 59-yard pass from halfback Grant Gillis and raced into the end zone. It was the longest touchdown pass in Rose Bowl history at the time—and the longest reported in major college football that season. An extra point attempt was again good, and Alabama took a 14–12 lead.

On the next possession, Washington fumbled on its own 30-yard line. It took just one play for Brown to score—this time on a pass from Hubert.

"Pooley told me to run straight up field as fast as I could, when I reached the 3-yard line, I looked back and sure enough the ball was coming over my shoulder," Brown said. "I took it in stride and went over (the goal line) carrying somebody. The place was really in an uproar."

The only downside was that Buckler did not make a third extra point, but it wouldn't matter. The Crimson Tide had scored three touchdowns in a blistering seven minutes of play in the third quarter. The team from Tuscaloosa took a 20–12 lead and left Washington reeling. By now, the crowd, most of them Californians, were wildly cheering the Crimson Tide.

Alabama so changed the tenor of the game in such a short period of time that it inspired sports writers to outdo themselves with a flourish of superlatives.

"With the desperate abandon of an almost forlorn hope, they threw the throttle wide open and cut the Husky defense to ribbons with a dazzling succession of passes, runs, and bucks," reported the *Associated Press*. "Hubert, here, there and everywhere, Johnny Mack Brown close at his heels, for the honors of victory, hoisted the ball across the Purple line thrice in rapid sequence and twice Buckler added the extra point."

Washington's Wilson returned to the game in the fourth quarter, desperately trying to rally his team. He threw a touchdown pass to cap an 88-yard drive and, combined with a successful extra-point try, closed the gap to one point. The Huskies would get one final, harrowing chance to win the game when Wilson took off around end and broke into the open field. Wade later recalled that he thought the Tide would lose the game right there as he watched Wilson run. But Johnny Mack Brown, who despite his brilliance on offense had been criticized by Wade for his defensive play when he had first showed up on campus as a freshman, made a stunning open-field tackle of Wilson.

"Give Johnny Mack Brown credit," said Hoyt "Wu" Winslett, an end on both the 1925 and 1926 Alabama teams, in a video included in the *Roses for Crimson* documentary.

"Johnny Mack brought him down, which I would have sworn one fellow couldn't do. But Johnny Mack by himself brought Al Wilson down and saved the ball game."

Alabama defeated Washington 20–19, launching celebrations not only at the Rose Bowl but across the American South. Crowds jammed into those theaters in Alabama joyously spilled out into the streets and were joined by thousands more.

"It was almost unbelievable what we accomplished," Winslett said.

Said Johnny Mack Brown: "We didn't just play for Alabama, but for the whole South."

As if to underscore that fact, the train carrying Alabama players home was greeted by cheering crowds throughout much of the journey. When they stopped in New Orleans, a thousand people—many of them Tulane students—were there to greet them. At Livingston, Alabama, a special player in Crimson Tide history—Bill Little, the man who brought football to the university back in 1892—was among those who welcomed them.

By the time they rolled into Tuscaloosa on January 5, several thousand were there to cheer them. Alabama had joined the elite of college football, not only lifting its own reputation, but also greatly improving the perception of southern football with it. Nothing would ever be the same, and even back on the West Coast, writers seemed to instantly know it.

"Tuscaloosa, Alabama, which Western fans didn't know was on the map, is the abiding place of the Pacific Coast football championship today," *The Los Angeles Evening Herald* reported.

It was the Crimson Tide's first national championship. And only the beginning.

6

A New Fight Song, a Return to the Rose Bowl, and a New Place to Call Home

Ethelred Lundy "Epp" Sykes enrolled at The University of Alabama in the fall of 1922 with $175 to his name, a deadpan sense of humor, and a penchant for music that seemed odd for a freshman interested in engineering.

"Among other accomplishments, he did things to a piano," wrote Arthur MacLean in the May 1926 issue of UA's renowned humor and literary magazine, *Rammer-Jammer*.

Sykes could also do things in a classroom, like finish near the top of his high school class academically, a trend he continued in college. So he "stayed here by the grace of God and the Alabama Power Company, which awarded him a four-year scholarship in the College of Engineering shortly after he entered the University," wrote MacLean.

Sykes got the most out of those four years, joining the Capstone Orchestra and the Glee Club, representing his fraternity—Phi Kappa Sigma—in the Pan-Hellenic Council, serving as a captain in the ROTC, and always making the university's Honor Roll. Because of it, he was inducted into every honorary organization available to him, including Tau Pi Epsilon (the engineering honorary fraternity), Omicron Delta Kappa, the Jasons, and the *Corolla* (yearbook) Board.

But it was Sykes's election as editor of *The Crimson-White* (the student newspaper that still used a hyphen in its name at the time) in the spring of 1925 that provided him with one of the campus's most influential platforms and raised his profile as a student leader. Yet, when Sykes was announced on A-Day that spring as the winner of the Pan-Hellenic Loving Cup as the university's most accomplished student—and *Rammer-Jammer* came calling to publish his biography—he joked: "I haven't any biography."

Like other UA students, and indeed, just about everyone across the southern United States who cared about football, Sykes got caught up in euphoria over the Alabama Crimson Tide's stellar 1925 season and that thrilling first-ever invitation to the Rose Bowl. But unlike most of the fans, Sykes and other staff members at *The Crimson-White*, the *Corolla*, and *Rammer-Jammer* had front-row seats from which to witness the transformation of the football program from just another decent southern team slogging through a tough schedule to an elite national power. To that extent, a consensus developed among the publications that the university needed a stirring new "football song," as *Rammer-Jammer* called it, to go with such an extraordinary program.

So in its November 1925 issue, *Rammer-Jam*mer announced a contest to replace the existing song—a variation of a Washington and Lee University tune called "Swing"—with a new football march that would be specific to Alabama's program and, it was hoped, would be as thrilling to hear as the Crimson Tide was to watch on the field.

It was a bold request that came with a $50 cash prize to the winning writer/composer. It also came with certain stipulations: "The words and music must be written by an alumnus, undergraduate, or instructor at the University of Alabama," wrote the *Rammer-Jammer* editors. "The manuscript must be original as to words and tune. . . . It is suggested that the tune of the song be a lively march air, similar to ones now used by other colleges. It is also suggested by RAMMER-JAMMER that the words be not over 16 or 20 lines."

The three judges included a popular music professor and director of the university's Glee Club and a nationally known Latin professor. Among those contributing to the $50 prize was Carl L. Carmer, an English professor and *Rammer-Jammer* faculty adviser who later wrote the national bestselling book *Stars Fell on Alabama*, and William "Champ" Pickens, an Alabama booster who was also the namesake of the trophy awarded to the winner of college football's Southern Conference. Pickens was credited, as well, with first coining the now-familiar name for Alabama's marching band. It seemed the band had given a rousing performance during a 1922 away game against Georgia Tech in Atlanta, even as Alabama's football team was getting routed on the field that day. The band sounded pretty much like a "million dollars" compared to the team's performance, Pickens is said to have told a sportswriter. Others, however, including *The Crimson-White* in a story published in 1929, credited "Atlanta football fans" at the 1922 game with the "million dollar" name. The fans had been impressed, the newspaper reported, with how well the 27-member travel group held its own against Georgia Tech's 88-piece band.

Whatever the real origin of the Million Dollar Band's name, one thing seemed certain: they were going to get a new fight song to play if the *Rammer-Jammer* contest was successful. Editors set an entry deadline of "before midnight" on December 15, 1925—which would turn out to be just 16 days before Alabama was scheduled to meet Washington in the Rose Bowl in California. Whether it was due to the Christmas and New Year's break, or simply because more time was needed, the deadline was pushed back to January 15, 1926, according to a later issue of *Rammer-Jammer*.

A two-part series of live performance trials was held beginning in early February, to pare down more than a dozen entries. The winner was announced in the April issue of *Rammer-Jammer*. It was called "Yea Alabama!" and it was written and composed by Epp Sykes, the engineering student who had won all those honors, had become editor of *The Crimson-White*, and was now about to be immortalized in Alabama football history.

Sykes, according to former University of Alabama system trustee Frank Bromberg Jr., wrote the song in one night, beginning on the house piano at his fraternity, Phi Kappa Sigma, and finishing on the Delta Kappa Epsilon fraternity's piano a few hours later. Bromberg's source for these details was his father, Frank Bromberg Sr., who was a lifelong friend, fellow student, and jazz band member with Sykes and was with him that night.

"Time was of the essence and the stakes were high," Bromberg Jr. wrote in a 1995 letter to Thomas J. Hamner Jr, author of the book *Strike Up the Million Dollar Band*. Moreover, Bromberg said his father mentioned that Sykes completed the song before the Rose Bowl, apparently working on the original *Rammer-Jammer* deadline.

"Sometime between the end of the 1925 season and the departure of the team for its January 1, 1926, game with Washington, the song was written," Bromberg said.

If so, that makes the lyrics Sykes wrote even more remarkable and reflected the sky-high anticipation that was brewing on campus, in the state, and throughout the South that December, as Alabama prepared to make history at the Rose Bowl. The song, as Alabama fans well know, emphasizes the importance of never forgetting the Rose Bowl.

In publishing the song and composition in May 1926, *Rammer-Jammer* editors noted they had "no power to make the student body accept the song. We do ask that the song be

Ethelred "Epp" Sykes, author and composer of "Yea Alabama!" (From the *Corolla*, courtesy of the UA Office of Student Media)

played on every occasion in which a battle march is needed, and, if it is liked, for the students to accept it."

As anyone who has ever attended an Alabama game in the 21st century can attest, and microphones and cameras from ESPN, ABC, or CBS can verify, "Yea Alabama!" has been far more than just accepted. It is one of the most well-known and iconic college football fight songs in America. Winning—and a good effort by a young but talented student back in the 1925–26 academic year—can do that.

Sykes lived long enough to see the impact of his song: he graduated later that spring of 1926, joined the Air Force, served in the Pacific in World War II, and later rose to the rank of brigadier general. Back in 1926, Sykes had used the $50 cash prize he won in the contest to pay for an arrangement to be published for the Million Dollar Band. Two decades later, he signed over his copyright of "Yea Alabama!" to the university. He died in 1967, but, as has often been said, music lives forever.

Another Undefeated Season and Back to the Rose Bowl

The Crimson Tide faced the 1926 season with a lot of confidence, but a boatload of questions, beginning with how to replace the biggest stars on the unbeaten national championship team a season earlier. Pooley Hubert, Johnny Mack Brown, Grant Gillis, Bruce Jones, Ben Hudson, Bill Buckler, and Pete Camp were all lost to graduation.

As it turned out, Wallace Wade and his team simply reloaded, running through the schedule in much the same way the 1925 team had done. The Crimson Tide opened the 1926 season at home on Denny Field with a blowout 54–0 win over nonconference Millsaps. Tolbert "Red" Brown, brother of famed halfback Johnny Mack Brown, raced to spectacular touchdowns of 92, 70, and 30 yards. A week later, Alabama got its first Southern Conference victory of the season with a hard-fought 19–7 win over Vanderbilt in Nashville. Next came a 26–7 victory over Mississippi State and a 21–0 shutout of Georgia Tech in front of 20,000 people in Atlanta. Only Sewanee, which was still a southern football power during the 1920s, would seriously challenge Alabama the entire regular season. Late in the fourth quarter in a scoreless game, the Crimson Tide blocked a Sewanee punt, with the ball tumbling out of the back of the end zone for a safety. It gave Alabama, which had earlier failed to score on multiple trips inside the 10-yard line, a 2–0 victory and preserved an unbeaten season. From there, Alabama routed LSU 24–0, got past Kentucky 14–0, and ended the season with blowout victories over Florida (49–0) and Georgia (33–6). The 9–0 regular season run lifted the Crimson Tide's winning streak to 20 consecutive games, best in the nation.

It also marked the third consecutive Southern Conference championship for Alabama, and the Tide placed a record five players on the *Associated Press*'s first-team All-Southern squad.

Alabama's outstanding end, Hoyt "Wu" Winslett, received the most votes from *AP* sports writers and was named captain of the team. Winslett would also receive All-American honors.

Unlike the waiting game Alabama had been forced to play at the end of the 1925 season, there was no delay this time. Wallace Wade had been told by Rose Bowl officials following the Tide's victory over Washington that if his team had another stellar regular season, they would be invited back to defend their championship in Pasadena. Alabama's 9–0 record in 1926, including six shutouts, guaranteed them a spot in the big game on New Year's Day 1927.

Their opponent would be undefeated Stanford, coached by the legendary Glenn "Pop" Warner. The Rose Bowl had expanded its seating capacity since the game a year earlier, but ticket prices for Alabama-Stanford skyrocketed among scalpers anyway, to as high as $50 a pair, an extraordinary price in the 1920s. Despite Alabama's victory over Washington in the 1926 game, Stanford was a heavy favorite. Ernie Nevers, the former star fullback for Stanford and now playing in the NFL, predicted a Stanford victory by no less than two touchdowns. West Coast sportswriters, who had been wrong a year earlier, also made the same mistake in predictions this time, expecting a big Stanford win.

It all simply motivated Alabama, and the result was another classic struggle between two great teams. Although the 1926 Rose Bowl had been broadcast via radio locally in Los Angeles a year earlier, NBC Radio decided to air this one coast-to-coast—giving the game a live national audience and greatly increasing the bowl's popularity.

Stanford scored in the first quarter on a 20-yard touchdown pass, taking a 7–0 lead that would last until late in the fourth quarter. With just four minutes left in the game, the Crimson Tide's Babe Pearce blocked a punt and took possession on Stanford's 14-yard line. Four plays later, Alabama's Jimmy Johnson scored on a run at the goal line. There was no overtime and no 2-point conversion play allowed in college football at the time, so Alabama had only one choice, to try and tie the game. The Tide lined up to kick the extra point and, expecting a fierce Stanford rush, resorted to some gimmickry: Emile "Red" Barnes, who called the signals on kicks, shouted "signals off," and Stanford's players reacted by standing at ease, apparently thinking Bama was not ready for the kick. The ball was snapped to Alabama's holder, Wu Winslett, and Herschel Caldwell kicked it through the uprights, with no rush whatsoever coming from Stanford's line. The kick lifted Alabama to a 7–7 tie before a record 57,417 spectators at the game. If there was ever an Alabama tie that felt like a victory, this was it.

Wrote the *Associated Press* in its coverage from the game: "Twice in two successive New Year's Day appearances in the Rose Bowl, the lads from the South have risen to real heights, last year to win from Washington and this year to hold the mighty Cardinals, bosses of the Pacific Coast Conference, to an even break."

Alabama players were welcomed for the second year in a row as returning heroes back in Tuscaloosa, and the Crimson Tide and Stanford both shared the 1926 national championship, as determined by a number of publications and rating services.

A New Home

By the beginning of the 1927 football season, Alabama was working on a 21-game unbeaten streak (including the 7–7 tie with Stanford). The Crimson Tide had played to enormous crowds on the road, including more than 45,000 in its first Rose Bowl appearance and more than 57,000 in the second. Yet, the team still didn't have a proper stadium for home games in Tuscaloosa. Since 1915, Denny Field (or University Field, as it was first called) had served as the team's home on campus, with a relatively small grandstand on the west side of the field and open space surrounding the end zones and east sideline for the thousands of other fans. Throughout this time, Alabama also continued to host "home" games at Birmingham's Rickwood Field and Montgomery's Crampton Bowl. (Alabama switched venues in Birmingham late in the 1927 season when a new 21,000-seat stadium, Legion Field, was opened on the city's west side. The stadium would later be expanded, and Alabama would continue to play many of its most noteworthy games there well into the 1990s.)

Beginning in 1929, however, the Crimson Tide finally got what the program deserved: A new 12,000-seat stadium, located on campus a couple of blocks west of Denny Field. Also named for UA President George "Mike" Denny, the new stadium opened with the Crimson Tide's 55–0 rout of Mississippi College on September 28, 1929. An official dedication came a week later in a 22–7 Homecoming victory over Ole Miss, when a capacity crowd of 12,000 showed up, despite threatening weather.

A series of major expansions over the next 80 years would bring the stadium, later renamed Bryant-Denny, to a capacity exceeding 101,000 people. But as Alabama's program entered the 1930s, it was enough that the football program, which still had more Rose Bowls ahead of it, had a fine new place to call home in Tuscaloosa.

Denny Stadium, circa 1929.
(From the *Corolla*, courtesy of the UA Office of Student Media)

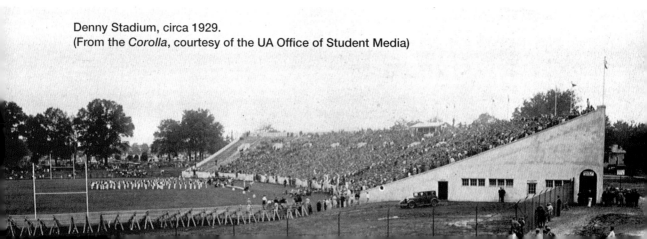

7

The 1930 National Championship: Alabama Builds on Its Legacy and Says Good-bye to a Great Coach

By the lofty standards that Alabama head coach Wallace Wade had established in Tuscaloosa, the 1927, '28, and '29 teams did not live up to expectations. They combined for a 17–10–1 record, and no championships, over three seasons—compared to the outstanding 27–1–1 mark set in the three seasons before them. Those teams, in 1924, '25, and '26, combined for three conference championships, two national championships, and two Rose Bowl appearances.

Despite the recent slump, and a growing bit of criticism from alumni, it was still surprising when Wade announced in April 1930 that he would leave Alabama to take over as head coach and athletic director at Duke University in 1931. Wade, according to news accounts at the time, gave no explanation for the decision, but privately those close to him said the coach was stung by criticism, considering what he had accomplished at UA. His relationship with President Denny was also said to be have been strained, particularly by what Wade considered to be Denny's interference in football decisions. But in later years, Wade indicated his decision was based on Duke's offer to allow him full control over athletics, and to work with him to incorporate the entire student body more fully into athletics through a strong intramural program.

Whatever Wade's reasons, he made it clear that he would honor the final year remaining on his contract and coach the Crimson Tide through the 1930 season. It would more than prove to be the right choice for both Wade and The University of Alabama.

It was evident from the very beginning of the season that the Crimson Tide had once again found the spark that would lead the team back to its place at the top of

Coach Wallace Wade. (From the *Corolla*, courtesy of the UA Office of Student Media)

the college football world. The Tide raced through its first three games (over Howard College, Ole Miss, and Sewanee), scoring a combined 132 points to 0 for its opponents. Next came an 18–6 homecoming victory over Tennessee, which ended a 33-game Vols unbeaten streak that dated back to 1926. It was the only game that Tennessee coach Bob Neyland and his team would lose in 1930. Alabama followed that landmark victory with a 12–7 defeat of Vanderbilt, and then a string of four shutout wins over Kentucky, Florida, LSU, and Georgia. Overall, the Tide's 9–0 record included seven shutouts— and one more was coming.

Alabama, led by halfback John Henry "Flash" Suther, sophomore quarterback Johnny "Hurri" Cain, and All-American tackles Fred Sington and C. B. Clements, was so good that Wade often started the second team in games. The "Shock Troopers," as the backups were called, more than held their own and were said to have never given up a single point.

The same strategy of starting backups would come into play in Alabama's next game, the biggest of them all: the Rose Bowl. It would be the Crimson Tide's third trip to Pasadena in six years. This time the opponent was the undefeated Washington State Cougars, which had outscored their nine opponents by a combined 218–56 margin. That trend would come to a dramatic end against Alabama.

New Year's Day 1931

A crowd of 65,000 showed up despite a slight, drizzling rain at Rose Bowl Stadium to watch the much-anticipated battle between Alabama and Washington State. The Crimson Tide was joined on the bench by former halfback Johnny Mack Brown, who had the lead role in the film *Billy the Kid* that fall and was well on his way to becoming a star in Hollywood westerns.

The Washington State Cougars may have done some acting on their own, showing up for the first time all season dressed "from head to toe" in red, with "even their shoes carrying out the crimson motif of their colors," wrote the *Associated Press*. "The gray skies above

Tournament of Roses

CAPTAIN FOOTS CLEMENTS of Alabama shaking hands before the battle with Elmer Schwartz of Washington State.

MONK CAMPBELL breaks away for a run that culminates into the third touchdown of the Rose Bowl Classic.

The officials of the game at Pasadena talking it over with the captains before the struggle.

CAMPBELL about to kick goal following his touchdown. He made it, of course.

Alabama in the 1931 Rose Bowl. (From the *Corolla*, courtesy of the UA Office of Student Media) made a perfect color combination for them. As the red hosts dashed out for the kick-off, 11 Mephistopheles seemed about to put on 'Faust' on a wholesale scale."

If the aim was to somehow send Alabama a message that the Cougars were the best "crimson" team on the field, it didn't work. Far more successful was Wallace Wade's starting tactic, sending out the Tide's second team Shock Troopers to start the game. They battled the Cougars to a scoreless tie by the end of the first quarter and no doubt sent a message that Alabama's backups were at least as good was WSU's starters. Once Wade sent in his first team in the second quarter, they made quick work of the Cougars, scoring 21 points in six minutes. Alabama's J. B. "Ears" Whitworth, who would years later serve as the Crimson Tide's coach, added a field goal in the fourth quarter.

"There was one writer on the coast who kept insisting Washington State would beat us by a field goal," Suther later told *Bowl Bama Bowl* book author and *Tuscaloosa News* sports editor Al Browning. "That kind of got away with coach Wade, so I think he had 'Ears' kick that field goal to rub it in a little. It was icing on the cake."

The Tide's 24–0 win was its most dominant performance yet at the Rose Bowl, and the team shared national championship claims with Knute Rockne's 10–0 Notre Dame team, which did not participate in postseason play but ended its season with a 27–0 victory over Southern California in Los Angeles' Memorial Coliseum. The Rose Bowl victory capped Wade's Crimson Tide career record at 61–13–3, including three national titles and four Southern Conference championships. Wade would go on to build Duke's program into a winner as well, compiling a 110–36–7 record there, along with six conference titles and two Rose Bowl appearances in 16 seasons. It is no surprise that Duke plays its home football games today in Wallace Wade Stadium.

In 1980, Wade, by then 88 years old, returned to Tuscaloosa for a reunion of his 1930 Crimson Tide team. Bama coach Paul "Bear" Bryant invited him to practice and introduced him to the team.

"Boys," Bryant reportedly said, "this man standing here is responsible for the great tradition of Alabama football."

8

Frank Thomas, Don Hutson, "the Other End," and Another Rose Bowl Crown

The soaring accomplishments of Wallace Wade's final Crimson Tide team in 1930 made the challenge that much tougher for the man who would replace him as head coach. Expectations were high. Yet, Wade knew exactly who could handle the job and suggested to UA President George "Mike" Denny that he could do no better than to hire Frank Thomas, the backfield coach (and associate head coach) at the University of Georgia.

If it seemed odd that Alabama should consider an assistant instead of a proven head coach to lead a program that had won two Rose Bowls, tied another, and gone unbeaten in three of the last six seasons, it made complete sense on closer inspection of Thomas's still-young career record. And after all, hadn't Wade been an assistant at Vanderbilt before Alabama hired him in 1923?

Frank Thomas actually had previously been a head coach, and quite a successful one at that, for four seasons at the University of Chattanooga (now The University of Tennessee at Chattanooga) beginning in 1925. He established a 26–9–4 record there, winning three conference championships at a school that had gone 14–19–4 in the four years preceding him. But much bigger things were in store for Thomas, who had seen firsthand what a top college football program could be back in 1920–1922, when he was a quarterback for legendary coach Knute Rockne's Notre Dame teams. During his first few months at Notre Dame, Thomas had roomed with George Gipp, the star player whose career and untimely death were immortalized in the 1940 film *Knute Rockne All-American*.

Thomas entered coaching as an assistant at Georgia in 1923 before taking the Chattanooga job and then, in 1929, returned to Athens as associate to UGA head coach Harry

Mehre. On July 26, 1930, nearly three months after Wallace Wade submitted his resignation, Alabama's athletic committee publicly announced Thomas's hiring. It was front-page news across the state the next day and made headlines, as well, in the sports sections of newspapers nationally. "Thomas To Coach Tide, 3-Year Contract Signed By Star Of Notre Dame," blared a main headline and subhead across the front page of *The Tuscaloosa News*.

In resigning back on April 30, Wade had committed to coaching the Crimson Tide through the 1930 season, making Thomas, perhaps, the nation's first "head-coach-in-waiting." It was also announced that Wade's stalwart line coach, Henry "Hank" Crisp, would become athletic director and also continue to serve as an assistant on the football team, ensuring continuity to the program, despite the change in head coaches. Though he was not yet in charge of the football team, Thomas traveled with Wade, Crisp, and the team to the Jan. 1, 1931, Rose Bowl, witnessing firsthand the Crimson Tide's blowout victory over Washington State.

Once the team returned from Los Angeles, Thomas formally took over the program and, when spring practices began, started the process of installing a new offense—transitioning the team from Wade's single-wing, unbalanced line attack to the offense Knute Rockne had taught him in South Bend, the Notre Dame box formation. That same spring, on March 31, 1931, word came that Rockne had been killed along with seven others in a plane crash in Kansas. It was a shocking and crushing blow to Thomas and other former Notre Dame players, many of whom had been inspired to follow in Rockne's footsteps and become college football coaches. It seemed the entire nation mourned with them. There was no bigger name in college football in 1931 than Knute Rockne.

Like so many other afternoon newspapers, *The Tuscaloosa News* rushed the news of Rockne's death onto its front page within hours of the crash. The *News* included a sidebar story with the headline: "Coach Thomas Almost Overcome with Grief."

"He was, as we all know, one of the outstanding figures of football," Thomas said. "It is a great loss to the game and to the coaches, as well as tremendous loss to Notre Dame."

Though his comments appeared stoic, the newspaper reported that Thomas was "too overcome to say more."

If tragedy and uncertainty surrounded those first few months of Thomas's tenure at Alabama, they would be replaced by what became an outstanding record of success, made even more remarkable because he had replaced such an iconic coach in Wallace Wade.

Thomas went 115–24–7 in fifteen seasons at Alabama. His Crimson Tide teams played in three Rose Bowls (winning two of them), went unbeaten three times, and won two national championships. They added victories, as well, in the Orange and Cotton bowls and also played in the Sugar Bowl, losing in a thriller to a 1944 Duke team that was without head coach Wallace Wade, who was in Europe, leading an Army battalion in

World War II. It bears mentioning that Thomas's teams also won four Southeastern Conference championships, including a title in the league's inaugural year, 1933.

For Thomas, it all began in his first game as Alabama's head coach on September 26, 1931. The Crimson Tide easily defeated Howard College 42–6 at home in Denny Stadium, with Hillman Holley rushing for 204 yards. There would be far more significant victories to come, but it was obvious from the first game that the new offensive scheme Thomas had originally learned at Notre Dame, and was now establishing at Alabama, was going to be a great success.

Eight more victories followed that fall, including several notable blowout wins, among them a 74–7 rout of Clemson, a 55–6 defeat of Ole Miss, a 53–0 romp over Mississippi State, and a 41–0 win over Florida. The Crimson Tide suffered just one loss, a crushing 25–0 defeat to Tennessee, which meant there would be no three-peat trip to the Rose Bowl. But overall, the team's 9–1 record and 36 points-per-game average during the season provided an excellent debut season for the new coach.

Following seasons of 8–2 in 1932 and 7–1–1 (including that first-ever SEC title) in 1933, Thomas and his team were ready to embark on what is still one of its most memorable seasons in Alabama history—a 10–0 run in 1934 that would include a Rose Bowl victory over Stanford, a fourth national championship for the program, a second consecutive SEC title, and a set of superstars in Millard "Dixie" Howell and Don Hutson. Both Howell and Hutson would not only become All-Americans, but would later be inducted in the College Football Hall of Fame. Hutson would also become an eight-time All-Pro selection receiver, would be inducted into the Pro Football Hall of Fame, and is still considered one of the greatest players in NFL history. For Alabama, the Howell to Hutson passing combination set the college football world ablaze with accolades in 1934. And Paul Bryant, the "other end" to Hutson on that same team, would make history of his own decades later, leading the Crimson Tide to six national championships and becoming the winningest major college football coach ever.

For Howell, Hutson, Bryant, All-American tackle Bill Lee, and so many other Bama standouts in 1934, the magical run to a national championship began just as coach Frank Thomas's first season three years earlier had started out, with a home victory over Howard College (now Samford University). Then came routs over Sewanee and Mississippi State, followed by a 13–6 victory over Tennessee at Birmingham's Legion Field, a 26–6 victory over Georgia, also at Legion Field, and a 34–14 win over Kentucky in Tuscaloosa. From there, it was sheer domination with shutouts over Clemson (40–0), Georgia Tech (40–0), and Vanderbilt (34–0).

An invitation to play Stanford in the January 1, 1935, Rose Bowl was waiting on the team when they returned to their hotel after the rout of Vandy. The Crimson Tide's preparation for the game began before the long train ride to Los Angeles, and, in fact, the train was delayed because of it. Thomas scheduled an early-morning practice on campus, just hours before departure.

Once in Pasadena, Bama players had the opportunity to meet some of the biggest names in Hollywood, including Lana Turner, Dick Powell, and Mickey Rooney, among others, and were also interviewed by the nation's top sportswriters — Grantland Rice and Henry McLemore, among them. A young radio reporter by the name of Ronald Reagan was also there, covering the Tide's practices at Occidental College.

Domination in Pasadena

The overflowing crowd that showed up for the Rose Bowl on New Year's Day was listed at 84,474, the largest audience in the game's history up until that point, and easily the most spectators to have seen either Alabama or Stanford ever play. The Indians, as they were still called then, were also undefeated, with a 9–0–1 record, including seven shutout victories.

Wrote Daven Dyer in *The Los Angeles Times*: "Alabama is the most impressive football squad I have ever seen come from east of the Rockies and Alabama is going to play the best Stanford team in history, a team as great as Southern Cal in 1931. If Alabama can beat Stanford, the Pacific Coast will give Alabama full credit for the greatest team ever to play in the Rose Bowl."

As it turned out, Dyer was prophetic. The Crimson Tide fell behind 7–0 early but came roaring back with 22 points in 13 minutes of the second quarter behind a furious passing and rushing attack. During that brief span, Alabama gained 150 yards passing—including a 54-yard touchdown pass from Dixie Howell's backup, Joe Riley, to Don Hutson and another 96 yards of passing from Howell to Hutson and Bryant—and 106 yards rushing. That included two Howell touchdowns, one on a spectacular cutback 67-yard run and another on an almost acrobatic, tackle-breaking 5-yard run to the end zone. The Tide took a 22–7 lead it would never relinquish.

After Stanford scored a touchdown in the third quarter, Howell connected with Hutson on a 59-yard touchdown pass in the fourth—sealing a 29–13 Alabama victory. Howell, alone, accounted for more yards than Stanford's entire team. It was a monumental win, showcasing the most prolific passing game the Rose Bowl had ever seen, and instantly ended talk among some West Coast fans and sportswriters that Minnesota, also undefeated, should have been playing in the Rose Bowl.

"I'd bet on 'em (Alabama) against Minnesota, the Chicago Bears, any Notre Dame or Southern California team, or any other team I ever saw," wrote Maxwell Stiles of *The Los Angeles Examiner*.

Wrote Ralph McGill of *The Atlanta Constitution*: "Not since the earthquake two years ago has California been so shaken. Alabama's 29-to-13 victory over Stanford this afternoon shook every seismograph in the state."

Like other writers, Grantland Rice, the most famous of them all, lavished praise on Howell, who gained 111 yards rushing, threw for 160 yards, scored two touchdowns on his own, threw for another, and punted six times for a 44-yard average. He also returned four kickoffs for 74 yards, giving him a then-Rose Bowl record of 345 all-purpose yards.

"Dixie Howell, the human howitzer from Hartford, Alabama, blasted the Rose Bowl dreams of Stanford today with one of the greatest all-around exhibitions football has ever known," Rice wrote.

A decade earlier, in the 1926 Rose Bowl, it had been the passing combination of Alabama's Pooley Hubert-to-Johnny Mack Brown that had amazed the crowd. This time, the Howell-to-Hutson combination drew even more accolades on the biggest stage in college football. Hutson's eight catches for 164 yards and two touchdowns offered a perfect glimpse of the player who would soon become the best wide receiver in professional football.

It was *The Los Angeles Times*'s Braven Dyer who might have best summed it all up: "The Tide was invited to California to put on a show, and they did it!"

9

Victory in World War II, and a Rose Bowl Win to Match

Most of the star players from the 1934 championship team were gone as Frank Thomas began preparations for the 1935 season. The departed players included Don Hutson, Dixie Howell, and Bill Lee, among others. If anyone ever doubted just how much talent was gone with them, one of those who returned—Paul Bryant—put it in perfect perspective, writing in his 1974 autobiography, *Bear: The Hard Life and Good Times of Alabama's Coach Bryant*, that if Hudson was still playing decades later, "there wouldn't be enough money in the bank to pay him, as good as he was."

Hutson was selected All-Pro eight times in his 11-year NFL career, was twice named the NFL's Most Valuable Player, was inducted into the Pro Football Hall of Fame, and in 1994, on the occasion of the NFL's 75th anniversary, was selected as one of the four greatest wide receivers in league history.

So it was understandable that Thomas and the 1935 Alabama team had some rebuilding to do, and it showed. They began the season ominously, playing to a 7–7 tie with Howard College, a team they usually blew out to start seasons. Overall, the team finished with a 6–2–1 record. It included a notable 25–0 victory over Tennessee in which Bryant, the "other end" to Hutson a year earlier, had one of the best games of his college career while playing with (no exaggeration) a broken leg. Bryant had suffered a fractured fibula in his right leg a week earlier in a game with Mississippi State and made the trip to Knoxville in a cast and on crutches. The team doctor took the cast off Bryant at the hotel the night before the game, allowing him to simply dress for the game at the request of Thomas, who thought it would help motivate the team.

Bryant, in a story recounted in the late Al Browning's book, *I Remember Paul "Bear" Bryant*, said he had not intended on playing, but once in the locker room, the Tide's line coach, Hank Crisp, got up in front of the team and said, "I'll tell you one thing. I don't know about you, you or you or you, but I know ol' Number 34 will be after them today." Bryant was wearing No. 34. "What could I have said?" Bryant recalled. "I just ran on out there."

After the season, Bryant became one of three Alabama players selected in the NFL's first-ever draft, but he was determined, instead, to be a coach, and Thomas thought so highly of him that he hired him as a fulltime assistant later in 1936.

"If your ambition is to coach, then coach," Thomas told him.

Alabama's 1936 team returned the program to national prominence with an 8–0–1 record (the only blemish coming in a scoreless tie with Tennessee) and a No. 4 national ranking in the *Associated Press* college football poll. Nonetheless, the Tide was not invited to any of the four bowls available then—Rose, Orange, Sugar, and the inaugural Cotton.

The next year, however, Alabama would return to the Rose Bowl following an undefeated 9–0 season and the team's third SEC championship in five years. But the West Coast would finally break through Alabama's unbeaten 3–0–1 Rose Bowl record. California defeated Alabama 13–0 on New Year's Day 1938. The Crimson Tide finished fourth in the final 1937 *AP* poll of sportswriters, which was released before the bowl games.

Over the next three seasons (1938, '39, and '40), Thomas and his Bama teams compiled a 19–6–2 record with no bowl appearances, but that would change in 1941. Less than a month after the December 7 Japanese attack on Pearl Harbor, Alabama met Texas A&M in the Cotton Bowl in Dallas, marking the Tide's first appearance in a postseason game outside of the Rose Bowl.

"The whole mood of the country was downcast," Holt Rast, the Tide's All-American end, said in *Bowl Bama Bowl*. "We knew we were in a war and I was kind of anxious to get the game and my college degree behind me so I could join up and help the country."

Alabama rushed out to a 29–7 lead and held on to a 29–21 victory over A&M in one of the most bizarre bowl games the team has played before or since. The Crimson Tide gained only one first down the entire game to 13 for the Aggies and had only 75 yards total offense to 309 for A&M. The difference was a never-ending string of A&M turnovers, including seven interceptions and five lost fumbles—12 in all. To Alabama's credit, the team took full advantage, scoring when the opportunities arose.

The win improved Alabama's 1941 season record to 9–2 and surprisingly earned them national championship recognition by the Houlgate System, a rating devised by statistician and sports publicist Deke Houlgate and primarily taking into account a team's strength of opposition. Though Alabama had lost to Vanderbilt and Mississippi State and finished third in the SEC during the regular season, it had been invited to the Cotton Bowl because of the strength of its schedule, which included victories over Tennessee, Georgia, Kentucky, Tulane, Georgia Tech, and Miami, among others.

"For the sixth time, a bowl game changed the national championship," Houlgate wrote in the 1954 edition of *The Football Thesaurus*, a compilation of college football statistics and information he published. "At the end of regular play it was all Minnesota, with Navy and Alabama in second and third. After the Crimson Tide beat the Texas Aggies, 29–13 (actually 29–21), in the Cotton Bowl, it was 'Bama, Minnesota and Navy ... in that order."

Minnesota, which finished 8–0 and did not play in the postseason, was named the 1941 national champion by the *Associated Press*. Once again, the *AP* final poll was released before the bowls. Alabama was ranked No. 20. But the Crimson Tide's No. 1 ranking by Houlgate was among five pre-Bear Bryant era national titles that a former Alabama sports information director, Wayne Atcheson, added to the Alabama football media guide in 1986. It remains the most controversial of the 17 national championships claimed by Alabama. The overwhelming majority of those titles, however, are beyond reproach. They are either *Associated Press* or Coaches poll titles, or championships won in the BCS and College Football Playoff national championship games. Alabama, for instance, has finished No. 1 a record 11 times in the *AP* poll since it began in 1936, followed by Notre Dame with eight first-place finishes.

The 1941 team may not have been awarded national championship rings at the time they played, but they and other players of their era were interested in something far more important—joining the nation's war effort. All told, more than 300 former University of Alabama players and coaches served in the military during World War II.

With the war on in Europe and across the Pacific, Alabama's 1942 football team completed a solid 8–3 season that included the team's first-ever appearance in the Orange Bowl on New Year's Day 1943. The Crimson Tide scored an impressive 37–21 victory over the favored Boston College Eagles, improving Alabama's bowl record to 5–1–1.

With so many players and students away at war, Alabama, like other college programs, did not field a team in 1943—one of only three years since the program started in 1892 that there would be no football in Tuscaloosa.

Thomas did his part at home, helping raise money for the war effort, serving on civic boards, and, when he could, preparing for a return to football in 1944. Once the university's athletic committee gave him the go-ahead, Thomas began assembling a team comprised in large measure by freshmen, who would be allowed to play varsity football for the first time due to so many upper classmen away in military service. One of the new recruits, Harry Gilmer, a 155-pound halfback, had gained notoriety at Birmingham's Woodlawn High School for his penchant of leaping into the air to pass, sometimes to get the ball over taller onrushing linemen, and other times because the acrobatics seemed to improve his accuracy downfield. Decades later, renowned players like Heisman Trophy winner Tim

Tebow at Florida would use the "jump pass," mostly near the goal line, but Gilmer was the trailblazer, and Alabama football would benefit greatly because of it.

Thomas and his "war babies," as he called them, mounted a commendable 5–2–2 record for the 1944 season that included a 19–0 upset victory over then-unbeaten Mississippi State in the last regular season game, followed by a 26–23 loss in a classic to favored Duke before nearly 72,000 people in the January 1, 1945, Sugar Bowl. Gilmer, the sensational freshman, played brilliantly in the game for Alabama, completing all eight of his passing attempts and nearly winning it at the end. Sports writer Grantland Rice called the game "one of the greatest thrillers of all time." Despite the loss, Alabama had become the only team to play in the Rose, Orange, Cotton, and Sugar bowls. The bowl tradition has continued in the decades since: by 2018 Alabama had played in 68 postseason games, more than any other team in the nation.

Harry Gilmer makes a leaping throw to Norwood Hodges against South Carolina during the 1945 season. (From the *Corolla*, courtesy of The University of Alabama Office of Student Media)

Emptying the Bench in the 1946 Rose Bowl

A year later, the "war babies" had grown up as Alabama prepared for the 1945 season, and it would be one to remember. It began with a 21–0 win over a Keesler Army Air Force team in front of 14,000 mostly-military personnel in Biloxi, Mississippi. Though Bama was never threatened in the game, the fact that Keesler's team kept the score relatively close may have had something to do with the muddy field conditions, and the fact that several players who had college experience suited up for Keesler, including a former Crimson Tide halfback, Johnny Hite.

Just 22 days earlier, on September 2, 1945, the Japanese formally surrendered to the US and allied forces, ending World War II. The mood in Tuscaloosa and across the nation was decidedly upbeat, and the Crimson Tide took inspiration from it. No team came closer than two touchdowns to Alabama during the season, and only Georgia did that (in a 28–14 Crimson Tide victory at Birmingham's Legion Field). That game featured two of the nation's biggest scoring threats in Alabama's high-flying halfback Harry Gilmer and Georgia's Charley Trippi. But it was Gilmer who ruled the day with three touchdown passes.

Overall, Alabama's margin of victories in 1945 underscored the strength of this team, led by Gilmer and All-American center Vaughn Mancha; fullbacks Norwood Hodges and Lowell Tew; quarterback Hal Self; ends Jim Cain, Rebel Steiner, and Dick Gibson; and tackles Tom Whitley and Francis Cassidy.

In addition to the victories over Keesler AAF and Georgia, the Tide steamrolled past LSU (26–7), South Carolina (55–0), Tennessee (25–7), Kentucky (60–19), Vanderbilt (71–0), Pensacola Naval Air Station (55–6), and Mississippi State (55–13).

In its 9–0 regular season run, Alabama's offense racked up a school-record 396 points (an average of 44 points per game) and allowed just 80 (an 8.8 average). Only undefeated Army, with 45.7 points per game, averaged more. The Cadets from West Point, led by Heisman Trophy winner Doc Blanchard, won the 1945 national championship, receiving all but one of 116 first place votes from sportswriters in *The Associated Press*'s final college football poll, released before the postseason. Alabama finished second, gaining that one outlying first place vote, and just one total point above third-ranked Navy, which lost 32–13 to Army in front of 102,000 fans and President Harry S. Truman in Philadelphia two days before the *AP* poll was released.

In the decades that have followed, more than one national sportswriter has concluded the 1945 Army team was college football's best ever, having routed six ranked teams. But the timing—1945 with the ending of World War II and the much-deserved outpouring of admiration for the nation's armed forces—certainly couldn't have hurt when it came time for writers to cast their votes. The silver lining, perhaps, for Alabama is that the Tide had risen from No. 7 in the first *AP* poll of the season to No. 2 in the final rankings.

If a national championship was not in the offing for Alabama, there was far more than a mere consolation prize awaiting. The Crimson Tide was invited to the Rose Bowl to face Southern California, which had won all eight of its previous Rose Bowl games, including the last two by a combined 54–0 over Tennessee and Washington.

The Trojans' perceived invincibility in the Rose Bowl as it headed into the annual game for the ninth time was the talk among West Coast sportswriters as soon as the matchup was announced. However, once the ball was kicked off in front of 93,000 fans on New Year's Day 1946, reality quickly set in. Gilmer and the Crimson Tide raced out to a 20–0 halftime lead and extended it to 34–0 in the fourth quarter before USC finally scored a couple of touchdowns after Frank Thomas had emptied the Bama bench. It was a mismatch so bad that USC didn't even make a first down until the third quarter. And it could have been far worse had Thomas not played everyone available to him.

"Southern California's Trojans went to the well nine times before they fell in, but that ninth time . . ." wrote Bill Becker of *The Associated Press*. "Never, say the oldest historians, has the Rose Bowl witnessed a more convincing shellacking than Alabama's alert, hard-hitting Crimson Tide gave the Trojans yesterday in exploding the myth of Southern California bowl invincibility."

The Tide totaled 351 yards (including 116 rushing from Gilmer) to just 41 for USC, holding the Trojans to just six yards rushing. The 34–14 victory gave Alabama a perfect 10–0 record, including a final 43-points-per game scoring average for the season, a school record that still stands today. It was also, in practical terms, the culmination of Frank Thomas's outstanding coaching career. "Coach Tommy," as many called him, had been fatigued for weeks, and battling high blood pressure, but he kept up a jammed schedule until ordered by his doctor to get more rest and give up cigarettes. His coaching skills, however, were as good as ever, as the Rose Bowl proved.

"There's a great coach," USC coach Jeff Cravath said, referring to Thomas, after the game. "I'll never forget what he did today. If he had wanted to name the score, he could have."

Coach Frank Thomas. (From the *Corolla*, courtesy of the UA Office of Student Media)

Norwood Hodges carries the ball with Hal Self and Rebel Steiner leading the way in the 1946 Rose Bowl. (From the *Corolla*, courtesy of the UA Office of Student Media)

The Rose was the fourth consecutive major bowl in which Thomas's Alabama teams had participated, no small feat then or now. But this would be his last bowl trip. Thomas's illness only seemed to worsen the following season, despite changes to his diet, bed rest, and other remedies the doctors had advised. His team finished with a 7–4 record in 1946, and he described it as his most difficult year in coaching. He resigned soon afterward, having already made private inquires with his former player, Paul Bryant, about succeeding him. It wouldn't work out that way, but the notion that Bryant could have arrived 11 years earlier than he ultimately did as Alabama's head coach is intriguing, to say the least.

Bryant had just finished his first year as head coach at Kentucky in 1946, leading the Wildcats to a 7–3 record, a considerable turnaround from the 2–8 record the season before he arrived. He had done much the same thing in a one-year stint as head coach at Maryland in 1945, guiding that team to a respectable 6–2–1 record compared to 1–7–1 without him a year earlier.

Bryant later wrote in *Bear* that he told Thomas he would accept an offer to coach Alabama but added that University of Kentucky President Herman L. Donovan then stepped in and refused to let him out of his contract. Donovan also gave Bryant a substantial raise and extended the terms of the contract at Kentucky from five to ten years.

Neither Bryant nor Thomas mentioned their discussions publicly at the time, and Thomas went on to recommended Harold "Red" Drew as his replacement. Drew had been an assistant coach with Thomas going back to the 1928 season at Chattanooga and had joined him in Tuscaloosa, as well. For the 1946 season, however, Drew had been hired as head coach at Ole Miss. He quickly accepted the Alabama job when it was offered, and a new era began with the 1947 season.

The soaring impact of Frank Thomas's tenure at Alabama could not be underestimated. His teams were consistently contenders at the highest level. Three of them went unbeaten, two of them won national championships, four of them won SEC titles, and overall, he had a stellar 115–24–7 record with the Crimson Tide, including a 4–2 major bowl record. He was inducted into the inaugural College Football Hall of Fame in 1951, and, on May 10, 1954, he died from illness related to his hypertension.

"The country at large has lost one of its best known and most admired men in college sports," said A. B. Moore, president of the NCAA and dean of The University of Alabama's Graduate School. "Coach Thomas served the University with all his heart and able mind on many fronts. More than any coach I have known, he had an active and intelligent interest in the entire institution."

10

Renewal of a College Football Rivalry

Harold "Red" Drew knew Alabama's football program as well as anyone, having served the better part of 15 years in Tuscaloosa as an assistant to Frank Thomas. Drew had been there alongside Thomas for three Rose Bowl appearances, including two dominating victories there and four SEC championships. He seemed entirely suited to the head coaching job at Alabama following Thomas's resignation in 1946.

Beginning in 1947, Drew would establish a respectable record 54–28–7 record over eight seasons, including his best year, a 10–2 run that concluded with an earth-shattering 61–6 blowout of Syracuse in front of live national television cameras in the January 1, 1953, Orange Bowl. He also led the Tide to an SEC title and two other bowl appearances—the 1948 Sugar Bowl and the 1954 Cotton Bowl. That Cotton Bowl became infamous as the game in which Alabama fullback Tommy Lewis came off the bench and tackled Rice halfback Dicky Moegle after he broke free down the sideline on what the referees ruled would have been a 95-yard touchdown. Moegle was awarded the score, and Rice won the game 28–6.

Drew's accomplishments as head coach, however, could not live up to the rare heights that Frank Thomas and Wallace Wade had established in Tuscaloosa, and because of it, there was criticism of the program. Drew would be forced to resign following the 1954 season, but the decline that had begun that year would only get worse—far worse—after he left.

One thing no one could criticize was Drew's record against Auburn once the cross-state rivalry was renewed in 1948 after a 41-year hiatus. Drew finished with a 5–2 record against the Tigers, with his Crimson Tide teams combining to outscore them 158–56 in those seven games. It all began with a rout for the ages.

Burying the Hatchet

More than 3,000 Alabama students, faculty, and fans gathered on the UA quad for a bonfire and pep rally on the evening of Thursday, December 2, 1948. It was less than two days before Alabama and Auburn would meet at Birmingham's Legion Field in the feverishly anticipated renewal of a series that few, if anyone, could accurately say why it had ever been discontinued in the first place. Underscoring the craziness that week was the fact that seven Auburn students had been arrested on Alabama's campus, charged with disorderly conduct—or more specifically, accused of plotting to light the UA bonfire hours before the pep rally.

"Two of the seven students were caught around a huge pile of trash arranged for a bonfire that will open the Alabama pep rally tonight," *United Press* reported. "Those two were tracked back to an automobile containing five other students. A quantity of gasoline and kerosene, presumably to be used in lighting the bonfire prematurely, was confiscated."

A December 8 hearing was set for the wayward students, but it was humiliating enough that they had royally flubbed the prank and found themselves in legal trouble in the process. So humiliating, in fact, that Tuscaloosa City Judge Joe Burns threw out the charges at the hearing, saying, "They have been punished enough," and fired off a letter to Auburn President Ralph Draughon informing him the students no longer faced charges. It seems that the faculty disciplinary committee at Auburn had recommended suspension for the students. In the quirky, topsy-turvy sort of relationship that would come to define the rivalry, it was no surprise that University of Alabama students also circulated a petition asking Auburn officials for leniency for the seven.

Other Auburn supporters, by the way, had been more successful in their pranks, painting their team's battle cry "War Eagle" on UA's Denny Chimes and "Auburn" across the white columns of the women's dormitory Tutwiler Hall. These graffiti artists at least had the good sense not to get caught.

Once Saturday arrived, the mood was decidedly upbeat in Birmingham, with thousands turning out just hours before the game for a parade featuring bands, cheerleaders, and cars decked out in either crimson-and-white or blue-and-orange streamers. The morning also featured a ceremony at the city's Woodrow Wilson Park in which the student government presidents from Alabama and Auburn dug a hole and buried a new hatchet that someone must have just bought in a hardware store.

While the "burying the hatchet" symbolism was laudable, it remained a fact that no one could pinpoint just why these teams had not met since a 6–6 tie in 1907. There had been arguments back then over everything from the size of travel squads, to per diem lunch pay for players, to officiating. But even the coaches and university officials from that era couldn't figure out why it had taken so long to bring these natural rivals back together.

The break "never made much sense" and was over "trivial things," said Mike Donahue, who had served as Auburn's coach in the years before and after 1907 but, as the school's athletic director, had taken a one-year hiatus away from coaching that year.

Attending Birmingham's Monday Morning Quarterback Club meeting the week of the renewal game, both Donahue and John (Doc) Pollard, Alabama's coach in 1907, disputed a sort of urban legend that the rivalry had been marred by fights between players in those years.

"I don't remember any game in which the playing was any cleaner than in the Auburn-Alabama games," Donahue said.

It was clear, however, that the game had been renewed only after state legislators threatened to cut funding to both schools if they didn't finally agree to meet again. The presidents of both schools met earlier in the year and formally agreed to schedule the game on December 4. It seemed, for everyone concerned, that 41 years was long enough. It was time to play.

The fact that neither team was having a great season did nothing to dampen the anticipation of the game. But Alabama, with a 5–4–1 record, was the clear favorite, and understandably so, considering Auburn's 1–7–1 mark. Still, what followed was a historic shellacking that no one had fully foreseen.

Led by quarterback Ed Salem, Alabama delivered a crushing 55–0 knockout that stands even today as the worst beating in the history of the Iron Bowl and exceeded a 53–5 whipping that Auburn had given Alabama way back in 1900. Decades later, in 2012, Alabama would come close to breaking the Iron Bowl margin of victory, sending in backups even before halftime of a 49–0 rout of Auburn to keep the scoring down. But the 1948 Alabama team could also have named its score, with Drew playing everyone available. Even a staggering 105 yards in penalties could do nothing to stop Alabama.

Overall, the Crimson Tide rolled up 404 yards of total offense, including 210 rushing and 194 in the air. For his part, Salem completed eight of ten passes for 159 yards and three touchdowns and scored another on a sweep around end. He also kicked seven consecutive extra points after touchdowns, before the Tigers finally blocked an eighth try. Alabama was just as dominating on defense. Auburn never made it past the Crimson Tide's 40-yard line and were held to just six yards rushing and a paltry total offense of 45 yards.

"When a fire gets started, it's mighty hard to put out," Drew said after the game. "We didn't figure to beat Auburn by that much, but everybody got in and everybody wanted to score."

It was Auburn's worst overall defeat since 1917, although Vandy had smothered them 47–0 just a month earlier. At least Auburn's band held up their part, putting on their share of what The Tuscaloosa News's Tom Little called "a dazzling demonstration" from both bands at halftime. But, as if to underscore the fanaticism of some of the fans when it comes to this great series, there was what amounted to a chase across the field just as Alabama's Million Dollar Band concluded their performance.

"An enthusiastic Bama supporter managed to grab the toy Auburn Tiger which was perched in front of the Plainsmen rooting section," Little wrote. "After a frantic foot race with the Auburn cheer-leaders, the Bama man finally made his way to the Crimson side of the field but the Tiger cheer-leaders trailed him over and rescued their mascot."

Their team, however, "didn't do nearly as well on the football field," Little noted.

Auburn coach Earl Brown didn't have much to say except the obvious: "Alabama is a fine football team and they played a fine game. I thought they were just as good this afternoon as Vanderbilt. They took advantage of every opportunity." But he added a comment that would come to characterize the most intense rivalry in college football: "There'll be another year."

Ralph Draughon, Auburn's president, said a few days after the game, "If I look emaciated and shopworn, it could be that I am still bleeding internally from the events of Saturday afternoon. I should like to say there are no alibis. I recall that when Gen 'Vinegar Joe' Stilwell came out of Burma, his only comment was: 'I claim we took a hell of a beating.'"

PART THREE

THE EPIC ERA OF
PAUL "BEAR" BRYANT

11

Mama Called

The shine on Alabama's storied college football tradition seemed to be wearing off fast as the 1954 college football season entered its final weeks. The Crimson Tide had started the season strong enough, winning four of their first five games, including victories over LSU, Vanderbilt, Tulsa, and Tennessee. But then the winning abruptly stopped. After two scoreless ties against Georgia and Tulane, the bottom completely dropped out. Alabama lost the last three games (against Georgia Tech, Miami, and Auburn) by a combined 71–7 points. The fact that Alabama scored only seven points in its last five games made a mediocre 4–5–2 season even less acceptable. Red Drew was forced to resign after eight seasons, though he would remain for years as head coach of the track team and an associate professor of physical education.

Today, there is a Red Drew Avenue near campus, just as there are streets named for other former Alabama football coaches. Drew never reached the success of his predecessors, Wallace Wade and Frank Thomas, but he is still held in high regard.

You're unlikely, however, to find any street named for Drew's successor, Jennings Bryan "Ears" Whitworth. And it's not that he wasn't welcome in Tuscaloosa. After all, Whitworth had been a tackle and placekicker on Alabama's championship 1930 and 1931 teams and even kicked a field goal in the Tide's 1931 Rose Bowl victory over Washington State. He had also served as an assistant for three years under Frank Thomas. Whitworth had gone on to become head coach of Oklahoma A&M (now Oklahoma State), compiling a less-than-stellar 22–27–1 record. Nevertheless, he was hired as Alabama's coach, replacing Drew after the university first made private inquiries during the 1954 season to Bear Bryant. Eight years earlier, Alabama had also made overtures to Bryant in replacing Frank Thomas, but, as Bryant later disclosed, the president of the University of Kentucky, where Bryant coached, would not let him out of a contract. This time Bryant, who was in his first year as coach at Texas A&M, would have none of it. He indicated in his auto-

Paul Bear Bryant in 1961. (From the *Corolla*, courtesy of the UA Office of Student Media)

biography, *Bear*, that he wouldn't consider being part of any attempt to remove Drew. "I wouldn't listen," Bryant said.

While Bryant set about rebuilding Texas A&M's program, Alabama suffered through the worst three-year run in its history—going 4–24–2 under Whitworth. It included a disastrous 0–10 record in 1955, part of a 20-game winless streak that stretched from the last half of the 1954 season (coached by Red Drew) through the first four games of the 1956 season.

It was time for another change. And Alabama again contacted Bryant, offering not only the head coaching job, but full control over athletics. Athletic Director Hank Crisp, who was also the longtime line coach for football and had recruited Bryant out of Arkansas' Fordyce High School, agreed to step aside, though Bryant insisted he wouldn't consider the job unless the university kept Crisp on in another capacity.

At a news conference in Houston on December 3, 1957, Bryant ended a month's worth of speculation in the media by confirming that A&M had agreed to release him from his contract and that he would become head football coach and athletic director at his alma mater, The University of Alabama. His reason for the move? "Mama called," he had told reporters earlier during all the speculation and essentially repeated it that day.

Hank Crisp was with him at the news conference, having flown in at Bryant's request.

In Tuscaloosa, officials read a statement from incoming UA President Frank Rose, who was being treated for a back injury in a Kentucky hospital and would officially assume his duties in Tuscaloosa on January 1: "We have secured in our way of thinking the best football coach in the country."

The announcement came on the same day that John David Crow, Bryant's outstanding halfback at A&M, won the Heisman Trophy. And, ironically, also the same day the *Associated Press* released its final college football rankings of 1957, naming Auburn as national champions. Auburn teams the past four years had slaughtered Alabama, winning by a combined 128–7 point spread. That kind of domination, and Alabama's deep slide as a program, were coming to an end.

On December 9, six days after this announcement, Bryant first met with Alabama players in Tuscaloosa, clearly defining his expectations in a twenty-minute talk. He told them that the past was over and forgotten, that it was time to commit themselves fully not only to winning football games, but also to excellence in everything they did—and that included studying hard, regularly calling their mamas, saying their prayers at night, and even making their beds. Nothing would be excused.

"If you're not committed to winning ball games, to making your grades, go ahead and get your stuff and move out of the dorm because it's going to show," he told them. "Pull out so we can concentrate on the players who want to play."

And he added: "I don't know any of you, and I don't want to know anybody. . . . I'll know who I want to know by the end of spring training."

Less than three weeks later, Bryant coached his last game for Texas A&M, a frustrating 3–0 loss to Florida in the Gator Bowl that Bryant and others attributed to the upheaval

Part Three

that his leaving had caused the Aggies. "It didn't take a genius to see nobody had any heart for the game," he later wrote.

By dawn on New Year's Day, Bryant was in his new office in Tuscaloosa, jump-starting the program that he would rebuild into one of the twentieth century's greatest college football powerhouses.

12

Worst to First

Paul Bryant took over the reins of his alma mater's struggling football program in 1958 with a well-earned reputation for winning at places that hadn't seen much of it in the years before his arrival.

In his one year at Maryland, he inherited a 1–7–1 team and led them to a 6–2–1 season. At Kentucky, he did some of his best work against a big obstacle: a nationally elite basketball program that seemed to suck the life out of the football program. No matter, Bryant won big there anyway, taking a neglected loser of a program and leading it to four bowls, an SEC championship, and finishing in the *Associated Press* final top 20 poll in five of his eight seasons. His best year at Kentucky, an 11–1 run in 1950, included a monumental upset of No. 1-ranked Oklahoma in the Sugar Bowl, ending the Sooners' 31-game winning streak.

Even today, Bryant's 60 wins is a record among Kentucky football coaches. At Texas A&M, he took apart the program in his first year, running off players who couldn't deal with his tough, some said brutal, "all in or nothing" approach, and by his third year led the Aggies to an undefeated 9–0–1 season and the Southwest Conference title. In his fourth year, which would be his last, his team reeled off eight consecutive victories and was ranked No. 1 by the *AP* sportswriters before word got out that he was considering leaving College Station to take the Alabama job. Bryant later said the speculation contributed to the team's three-game slide at the end.

"We would have won the national championship in 1957 if it hadn't leaked that I was going to Alabama," Bryant said in his autobiography. "The leak fouled up everything."

The University of Alabama's young new president, Frank Rose, had called Bryant "the best coach in the country" on the day both Bryant and UA announced his hiring. No one seemed to doubt that, given Bryant's record. But that didn't make the job he faced in Tuscaloosa any less challenging. He was not inheriting one of those legendary Rose Bowl teams like the one he had played on back in the 1934 season. Far from it; the bottom had completely dropped out of the Alabama program.

Gone were the undefeated seasons, the conference championships, and the adulation of those thousands of fans lined up to greet the conquering football heroes arriving back on the train from Los Angeles. This was a far different Crimson Tide program—one that had won just four games in three years. One that, during that same span, had ingloriously set a school record of 17 consecutive losses, part of a 20-game winless streak (including two ties).

None of it mattered now to Bryant. He wasted no time assembling a staff of assistants he trusted, and most of whom either played for him, had coached with him, or both. An immediate concern was recruiting, and Bryant knew just the man he wanted to have working with Hank Crisp on identifying and then going after top high school prospects. It was Jerry Claiborne, one of Bryant's former halfbacks at Kentucky, who had since worked as an assistant with him at Kentucky and Texas A&M.

As author Tom Stoddard wrote in his 1996 book, *Turnaround*, "Working closely with Crisp, Claiborne hit the recruiting trail and arranged for Bryant to talk by phone to blue chip players considering Alabama."

The result, as Stoddard mentioned, "turned out to be outstanding." Alabama signed a class that would become the foundation for Bryant's first national championship. Among the players were Billy Neighbors, Pat Trammell, Tommy Brooker, Jimmy Sharpe, Billy Richardson, Bill Oliver, Bill Rice, and Mal Moore.

Bryant also quickly completed the rest of his coaching staff: Carney Laslie, a former Bama player who was an upperclassman in Bryant's freshman year, had worked with him throughout the head coach's career so far and was now brought in as assistant athletic director. Phil Cutchin, a former Kentucky player who coached with Bryant both in Lexington and at Texas A&M, was named offensive coach. Pat James, who played for Bryant at Kentucky and joined his staff at A&M, now also followed him to Alabama as line coach.

Gene Stallings and Bobby Drake Keith, two of the "Junction Boys," so called because they were among the A&M players who managed to survive Bryant's infamously grueling summer camp in the 100-degree heat of Junction, Texas, in 1954, now followed him to Alabama as assistant coaches. Together with other assistants, Sam Bailey, Hayden Riley, Bobby Luna, and trainer Jim Goostree, this was a staff that not only would help Bryant win national championships, but several would become head coaches in their own right later.

Next, there was the business of winning football to attend to, and though Bryant had clearly spelled out in player meetings what he expected of them, few, if any, fully understood just how much he meant it. It began with closed-door, off-season conditioning drills in the third-floor gymnasium of the athletic dorm, Friedman Hall, that became so physically demanding and mentally tough that players considered them survival tests. A significant number of them from J. B. "Ears" Whitworth's tenure quit even before spring practices began. These were still the days when Bryant had a well-deserved reputation for running off players so that he was only left with those he absolutely knew wouldn't quit on him in games.

"I think at one time or another, every one of us wanted to quit," Mal Moore, a freshman on the team, said in 2008 on the 50th anniversary of that first Bryant year. "I had never been out of the town of Dozier (Alabama). But somehow, you'd hang in there for another day, another week and somehow you had made it through the semester. You just became more comfortable. A lot of players went other places, but that was all a part of making that big change and changing the way a team thinks. When you look back on it, it was remarkable."

Moore became a longtime Bryant assistant coach and later, the director of athletics at Alabama. He died in 2013, after playing a major role in another resurgence of Crimson Tide football. In 2007, it was Moore who hired Nick Saban, the man who has since matched Bryant's record of six national championships.

But in 1958, Bryant had yet to win his first one. It would come soon enough, but not before he had to establish the kind of discipline, organization, and entirely new system that didn't sit well with a lot of the players from the Whitworth days.

Once spring practices began in 1958, it was also clear how different things would be with Bryant in charge. Practices would be obsessively organized down to the minute, divided into specific segments or sets, and drills would continue until players got it right. If they couldn't get it done, they might just be told to collect their bags and leave. For good. There would be no standing around, absolutely no taking a seat on the field, and aside from the intense physical demands the players knew were coming, they would be challenged mentally more than they could possibly have realized. More than a few would not last through that spring.

Whereas Whitworth's practices, according to players, were more loosely organized and could run on for hours, Bryant's practices were two hours and fifteen minutes of sheer intensity. From the beginning, Bryant loomed over practice in a makeshift wooden tower (it would later be replaced with a permanent one), famously coming down and personally attending to players he saw not getting it right. No one, as both players and coaches would later say, wanted to see him walking down that tower.

"People often ask me if Coach Bryant ever came down out of that tower during practice," Jerry Duncan, who played for Bryant at Alabama in the mid-1960s, told *Southern*

Living magazine. "Believe me, you wanted him to stay up there. Because when he came down, the fur was about to fly."

By the time fall camp began, even more players had left and more would follow under the weight of intense two-a-days in the searing Alabama heat, and the constant, never-let-up pressure from the coaches.

"The riffraff are fast eliminating themselves and we had two good scrimmages," Bryant told the *Associated Press* one day during camp.

For the players who made it through, the reward would be a 1958 season that may not sound like much, with a 5–4–1 record, but it sure beat anything that had come before it in the Whitworth years. In fact, it was Alabama's first winning season in five years, stretching back to 1953, Red Drew's second-to-last year.

The conditioning paid off in ways that would come to characterize Bryant's early Alabama teams. Tide players were often outweighed 20 to 30 pounds by their opponents but made up for it in quickness, skill, better training, and far better conditioning than the teams they faced on Saturdays.

The next season, 1959, Alabama improved to 7–2–2, beat Auburn for the first time in five years, and went to the Liberty Bowl (located in Philadelphia at that time), the Tide's first bowl trip in five years. Though Penn State would win that one 7–0, it became the first of 25 consecutive bowls Alabama would play, 24 of them with Bryant as coach. His first year, 1958, would be the only season any Bryant-coached Alabama team wasn't invited to a bowl. Before he retired at the end of the 1982 season, Bryant would compile a 232–46–9 record over 25 seasons at Alabama, an .824 winning percentage, remarkable for such a long tenure as coach.

His record would include six national championships, 13 SEC titles, and enough stories to fill a library's worth of books. Overall, Bryant retired with a record of 323–85–17 in a 37-year career, making him the winningest coach in college football history at the time of his death in 1983.

But at the beginning of the 1960s, he was still just getting started at Alabama. The 1960 team went 8–1–2, beat Georgia Tech for a third consecutive year, beat Auburn for the second year in a row, and finished in the top 10 of the AP rankings for the first time since 1952. A 3–3 tie with Texas in the Bluebonnet Bowl did nothing to derail the freight train of a football team that Alabama and Paul Bryant would put on the field in 1961.

Total Domination and a National Championship in 1961

It wasn't that no one had any idea this was coming: after all, Alabama began the 1961 season ranked No. 3 in the *Associated Press* preseason college football poll—the team's highest ranking since 1945. But national sportswriters by now were well aware of the transformation going on in Tuscaloosa. Still, it was impossible to know, as the Crimson Tide took the field for its opener against Georgia in Athens on September 23, 1961, that no team would come within a touchdown of Alabama during the entire regular season. In fact, only 25 points would be scored against this team the *entire year.* (Compare that to the 256 points that J. B. Whitworth's team had given up in the disastrous 0–10 season of 1955.)

Paul Bryant, not known for hyperbole, was effusive in his praise for the 1961 defense. "I said that year that defense wins, and that's right," Bryant wrote in his autobiography. "We weren't just a good defensive team, we were a *great* defensive team. We led the nation in almost every category."

Led by quarterback Pat Trammell, two-way lineman Billy Neighbors, and Lee Roy Jordan, who played center and linebacker, Alabama easily dispatched Georgia 32–6. Next, they got past Tulane (9–0), crushed Vanderbilt (35–6) and North Carolina State (26–7), beat Tennessee in a rout, 34–3, for the first time since 1954, and then reeled off five consecutive shutouts: 17–0 over Houston, 24–0 over Mississippi State, 66–0 over Richmond, defeated Georgia Tech for the fourth consecutive year 10–0, and finished the regular season with a 34–0 shellacking of Auburn.

Both the *Associated Press* and *United Press International* released their final rankings three days after the Alabama-Auburn game. The Crimson Tide was No. 1, winning the program's first national championship under Bryant and signaling to the college football world that Alabama was back, and bent on staying there.

Cheerleaders lead Bama onto field before the 1961 Alabama-Georgia Tech game. (From the *Corolla,* courtesy of the UA Office of Student Media)

Part Three

Bryant helps his injured QB Pat Trammell off the field. (From the *Corolla*, courtesy of The University of Alabama Office of Student Media)

On December 5, the same day the final wire service polls were released, President John F. Kennedy paid tribute to the Crimson Tide at the National College Football Hall of Fame banquet, a black-tie event emceed by Bob Hope, at the Waldorf-Astoria Hotel in New York. Bryant, Trammell, and UA President Frank Rose were there to accept the National Football Foundation's MacArthur Bowl, named for Gen. Douglas MacArthur and awarded each year to the national college football champion. MacArthur, then 83 years old, presented the trophy to Bryant, Trammell, and Rose.

And the awards didn't stop there: The National Association of Coaches named Bryant Coach of the Year. Billy Neighbors was unanimously selected as an All-American, and Trammell and Lee Roy Jordan were second team picks. Trammell also finished fifth in Heisman Trophy voting.

Once the awards were done with, the Crimson Tide got back to work in preparation for a New Year's Day battle with No. 9 Arkansas in the Sugar Bowl in New Orleans. Alabama took a 10-point first half lead, and that's all it would need, winning 10–3 to complete an undefeated, 11–0 season. All told, Trammell and his teammates had outscored the opposition 297 to 25—a staggering accomplishment in a landmark year for Alabama football.

Trammell would go on to medical school and become a physician, but his young life was cut short by cancer in 1968. He was just 28 years old. Bryant, who had immense respect for his quarterback, never got over Trammell's death.

"You'll have to forgive me here for getting sentimental, but Pat Trammell was the favorite person of my entire life," Bryant wrote. "As a leader, I have never had another one like him."

Part Three

13

The Kid From Beaver Falls

The Alabama football team that gathered on the practice field in the heat of a 1961 summer included some of the best players in the nation, and they would go on to prove it that fall with an undefeated season and a national championship. They weren't exactly choir boys, as opponents would find out, but they all looked the part, sporting either crew cuts or short-cropped hair. So when a long-haired, lanky kid wearing sunglasses, a tight-fitted brown suit, and a straw fedora hat with a large white feather sticking out of the brim, and chewing on a toothpick, showed up at practice one day that August, he drew plenty of attention.

"I looked over to one of the graduate assistant coaches and I said, 'Who is that character?'" recalls former Alabama center Gaylon McCullough in the HBO documentary *Namath*. "'That's your new quarterback,' and I laughed and said, 'He'll last here about two weeks at the most.'"

Even more shocking to the players sweating through drills that day, Coach Paul "Bear" Bryant, surveying practice as usual from 25 feet above in his tower, picked up a bullhorn and told assistant coach Howard Schnellenberger to send the kid up the narrow, spiral staircase.

"The entire four years I was there, I never saw another player go on the tower with him," McCullough said.

Soon enough, it would be clear just who this kid was, and why he had been asked to ascend Bryant's tower. Joe Willie Namath, a late freshman signee from the industrial town of Beaver Falls, Pennsylvania, would become the best quarterback Alabama has ever had, and go on to skyrocketing fame in professional football. For now, though, he faced the daunting task of not only surviving in Bryant's regimented, unforgiving system, but also in handling the culture shock of his new home.

"He was literally dropped in here, almost like parachuted into a foreign land, so to

77

speak," McCullough, now a prominent plastic surgeon in Alabama, said in *Namath*. "You know, he was 'a Yankee.' He was different from the rest of the good old boys."

Namath had been recruited heavily by some of the best football programs in the nation following a sensational senior year in which he led Beaver Falls High School to an undefeated season and the Pennsylvania 2A state championship. A three-sport star, Namath had been offered a substantial amount of money to play baseball and skip college. But his mother and older brother insisted he get an education. He finally settled on the University of Maryland's program but failed to score high enough on his SAT for eligibility there. Not wanting any of their traditional rivals to sign Namath, Maryland coaches informed Alabama that he was available. Bryant immediately sent Schnellenberger to Beaver Falls. It took more than a week, during which time Schnellenberger ran out of expense money and wrote a couple of checks he knew his bank account couldn't cover until payday, but the assistant coach who would one day build the Miami Hurricanes into a powerhouse football program brought Namath back with him to Tuscaloosa.

The rest is Alabama football history.

What Namath may have lacked in grades, he expertly made up for in understanding the complexity of leading a football team. That included recognition of defensive alignments, getting his teammates where they needed to be, and having the ability to change plays at the line of scrimmage. He also, as the football universe would find out, had a rocket arm and a quick release. Bryant would later call him the most naturally talented quarterback he had ever seen.

What fans around the nation who would later watch as Namath led the New York Jets to a landmark 1969 Super Bowl victory might not have known is that he also had an outstanding ability to run the football during his early college career at Alabama, before knee injuries took much of that away.

The full range of Namath's talents was obvious from his first game, as quarterback for the Crimson Tide's freshman team, or the "Baby Tide," as they were called. (Freshmen were not eligible to play varsity football at that time.) On September 25, 1961, Namath carried the ball 13 times for 63 yards, including an 8-yard run for a touchdown in a 20–14 victory over Mississippi State's freshmen team. He also completed 7 of 11 passes for 44 yards and one TD. Not a spectacular passing performance, but that would come, beginning with his next game.

On October 8, 1961, *The Tuscaloosa News* described Namath's second game this way: "Passes from Alabama freshman quarterback Joe Namath filled the air at Denny Stadium Saturday afternoon as the Baby Tide took its second straight victory of the season, 32–6, over the visiting Tulane freshmen. Bama scored in every period. Namath dominated play throughout the game, directing an offensive attack that couldn't be stopped."

Namath's freshman team would finish with a 7–7 tie down at Auburn in a game in which he threw a 46-yard touchdown strike for his team's only score. Meanwhile, Alabama's varsity team, led by senior quarterback Pat Trammell, was demolishing opponents en route to the 1961 national championship.

Soon enough, Namath would get his chance to lead the Crimson Tide. It came on the opening game of the 1962 season when, in his first varsity start, he threw three touchdown passes in just three quarters of work to lead Alabama to a 35–0 blowout of Georgia at Birmingham's Legion Field.

From there, Namath and the Tide reeled off seven more consecutive victories, taking an 8–0 record and the No. 1 ranking into a November 17 battle with Georgia Tech in Atlanta. It was an annual meeting that was becoming more bitter by the year, particularly after a brutal injury a year earlier in which a Tech player had suffered a broken jaw and several teeth knocked out on a block by Alabama linebacker Darwin Holt. An article in the *Saturday Evening Post* magazine, written by Atlanta sportswriter Furman Bisher and titled "College Football is Going Berserk," alluded to the incident as evidence that Bryant was teaching brutality to his players.

The article was published less than a month before the 1962 Alabama-Georgia Tech game. (By the next January, Bryant would file a libel lawsuit against the *Post's* parent company, Curtis Publishing.) Alabama, which had won four consecutive games against Tech and carried a 19-game winning streak into the game, lost 7–6, failing on a two-point conversion try that would have won it.

Though the national championship was now out of reach, Namath and the No. 5-ranked Tide finished with a 38–0 rout over Auburn and manhandled No. 8-ranked Oklahoma 17–0 in the New Year's Day Orange Bowl game attended by President John F. Kennedy. Alabama's All-American linebacker, Lee Roy Jordan, had an astonishing 31 tackles in the game.

As Namath and Alabama prepared for the next season, long-simmering racial turmoil at the still-all-white University of Alabama came to a head. On June 11, 1963, Alabama Gov. George Wallace stood in front of the doorway to the university's Foster Auditorium in a staged attempt to stop two black students, Vivian Malone and James Hood, from enrolling. After a statement of defiance, Wallace gave way to federal officials and stepped aside, allowing the two students to enroll.

For Namath, who had attended integrated schools and played on sports teams with black students back in Beaver Falls, segregation was about as foreign as anything he had seen.

"I wasn't really aware of how segregated the South was," he said in the HBO documentary *Namath*, describing his surprise at the depth of the racial divide in the South when he first arrived on campus. "You can't drink out of a water fountain? You can't sit at a counter and order food? You're different? Why? Your color?"

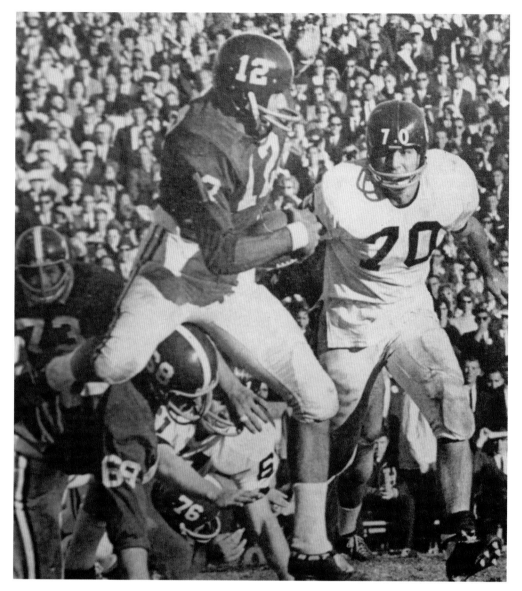

Joe Namath in the backfield in 1963. (From the *Corolla*, courtesy of the UA Office of Student Media)

Namath said he was just 30 to 40 feet away when Wallace stood in the door and could hear "every word. . . . Vivian went in, man, and that was special. Those of us that understood had goose bumps first, and it was a big change."

Once the 1963 season started, Namath and Alabama appeared ready for another run at the national title. But it was not to be. The Tide finished with a 9–2 record that included a 17–7 victory over Ole Miss in the Sugar Bowl. Backup quarterback Steve Sloan, not Namath, led the Tide in the last two games. Bryant, underscoring that no player was above team rules—including his star quarterback—suspended him for the final two games

Joe Namath against Auburn, 1963. (From the *Corolla*, courtesy of the UA Office of Student Media)

against Miami and the Sugar Bowl matchup with Ole Miss. Namath's violation, not disclosed publicly at the time, was drinking alcohol after a game.

"Being a part of the team is a privilege, not a right," Namath later said in his autobiography. "He [Bryant] made me a better person."

Determined to get his starting job back the next year, Namath buckled down and rededicated himself to the team. Both he, Bryant, and the entire Alabama program would be the better for it.

14

"Ten Years Off My Life"

A *Saturday Evening Post* magazine article titled The Story of a College Football Fix exploded into the Alabama football program like a missile strike in March 1963. It accused Bear Bryant and Georgia athletic director Wally Butts of conspiring to fix the September 22, 1962, Alabama-Georgia football game.

"Not since the Chicago White Sox threw the 1919 World Series has there been a sports story as shocking as this one," began a lurid editor's note introducing the article. "This is the story of one fixed game of college football. . . . The corrupt were two men—Butts and Bryant—employed to educate and to guide young men."

The story alleged that Butts had passed along Georgia plays, formations, player tendencies, and strategy to Bryant in a telephone call nine days before the game. An Atlanta insurance salesman, George Burnett, said he overhead the call and took notes. Burnett said he had inadvertently been cross-connected into the call between Butts and Bryant when he dialed a number at the office of an Atlanta public relations firm. Butts, it turned out, was making the call to Bryant from that office.

Alabama, a 14- to 17-point favorite going into the game, won it 35–0. Crimson Tide players later said they saw and heard nothing during practice or the game to indicate any kind of a fix was remotely possible. Had Bryant and Butts, for instance, been conspiring to fix the game so that the Tide covered the betting line, then why had Bryant decided to lift his starters leading 28–0 in the third quarter, risking the possibility that Georgia, playing against Bama backups, might score enough points to ruin the bet? Though Butts had been forced out as head football coach at the end of the 1960 season, and kept on as athletic director, there seemed little or no incentive for Bryant to risk his entire career on a game that Alabama clearly was expected to win big and didn't need any help doing it.

The *Post* paid Burnett $5,000 for the story, another $500 each to his lawyer and a business partner, and assigned a freelance sports reporter, Frank Graham Jr., to write it. Furman Bisher, the Atlanta writer who had penned a college football brutality story for the *Post* the previous October, calling into question Bryant's coaching tactics, reportedly provided supporting quotes for the new story. It was a development that did not help the *Post*'s claim of objectivity, considering Bryant had since already filed a lawsuit over Bisher's brutality story.

The fix story hit newsstands on March 23, 1963, but galley proofs of the article had circulated well ahead of that time, and both Bryant and Butts went on television to vehemently deny the charges.

"Never in my life have I ever attempted to fix or rig a ball game, either as a player or as a coach," Bryant said in a statewide television address in Alabama on March 17. "Certainly such charges have been derogatory to my integrity and character, but not only to myself but to the University of Alabama . . . but one of the worst things to come of this is that it is a reflection on the performance of the University of Alabama football players. . . . Ladies and gentlemen, I have nothing to hide."

All three central figures to the story—Bryant, Butts, and Burnett—passed lie detector tests, and both Bryant and Butts immediately filed lawsuits against the magazine's parent company, Curtis Publishing (with Bryant adding an additional $10 million to the $500,000 suit he had brought against the company over the brutality article back in October).

"How much is a year of a man's life worth?" Bryant wrote in *Bear*. "I don't know, but *The Saturday Evening Post* took ten years off my life, and I billed them $10 million for it. I guarantee you, if I had collected that much—which I didn't—it would not have paid for the suffering they put me through."

Butt's trial was scheduled first, beginning on August 5, 1963, in a federal courthouse in Atlanta. Bryant was the star witness for Butts's case and made a lasting impression on the jury, as James Kirby, a law professor serving as a legal observer for the SEC commissioner's office, later wrote.

"It was a virtuoso performance, and its effect was enormous," Kirby wrote in his 1986 book, *Fumble: Bear Bryant, Wally Butts and the Great College Football Scandal*. "Bryant's denials of guilt could not have been more forcefully delivered."

Curtis Publishing's attorney didn't stand a chance in the courtroom against Bryant, Kirby wrote: "On cross-examination, Wellborn Cody did not score a single point. Bryant showed Cody the same contempt he had just shown those responsible for the *Post* article. At several points Cody was visibly taken aback by the ferocity of Bryant's answers."

Ultimately, the jury believed Bryant and Butts's assertion that the information scribbled in notes by Burnett was common knowledge in football, represented no "secrets," as the *Post* had claimed in its article, and the conversation between them amounted to a routine call made between coaches and athletic directors. Worse, for the *Post* and its parent company, it was disclosed at trial that while Burnett did take notes, and apparently heard the actual conversation with Bryant and Butts, the writer never saw Burnett's notes. Burnett also disputed a quote attributed to him in the story.

The jury awarded Butts $60,000 in general damages and $3 million in punitive damages, although the award was later reduced to $460,000. Bryant settled out of court with Curtis for $320,000.

"Hindsight is better than foresight, every time, and maybe I'd be $2 million richer or even the full $10 million richer if I'd stuck it out," Bryant wrote. "Today I would. Then I couldn't. I doubt I'd be alive to collect if it had gone on any longer, all it was taking out of me and my family."

The irony, it seemed, was that while the *Post*'s article predicted careers would be ruined by the scandal, it was the magazine itself that met a quicker-than-anticipated end, shutting down publication in 1969 (though it would later be brought back in a different format and published six times a year by a new owner).

For Bryant and his Alabama teams, there were many more SEC and national championships to be won. The darkest chapter in his life was over for good.

Part Three

15

Broadway Joe, a National Championship, and Heartbreak in Miami

Joe Namath opened the 1964 season in fine form, running for three touchdowns and completing 16 of 21 passes for an efficient 167 yards in a 31–3 Crimson Tide rout over Georgia at Denny Stadium in Tuscaloosa. It was an impressive return to action for the Alabama star who had been forced to sit out the final two games of his junior season due to team rules violations. The message had been clear to the entire team: if Paul Bryant could suspend the best quarterback he ever had for two critical games to end a season, it might be a good idea for everyone to pull together and stick to the plan.

"Namath was the big difference throughout the game," said Vince Dooley following his first game as Georgia's head coach. "He is just great. He picked us to pieces."

Next came a 36–6 dismantling of Tulane down in Mobile's Ladd Stadium, followed by a 24–0 shutout of Vanderbilt at Birmingham's Legion Field. Namath had continued to score with both his passing and running, not only playing the best football of his Alabama career, but also providing the bulk of the Crimson Tide's offense.

But in the next game, against North Carolina State, Namath's days as a dangerous runner would come to an end. On a third-and-one play, Namath rolled out to his right, then cut back to avoid defenders. "I must have hit a bad spot on the field because my knee just snapped," he wrote in his autobiography. "The movement of it—I felt the thing kind of cave inward. It was so sudden; it reminds me of when I hear people describe being shot. I was never shot; I don't know what that's like. But it was going from one instant you're fine and the next you're engulfed in pain."

No one could fully know it at the time, but it would be the first of a series of knee injuries that would plague Namath the rest of his brilliant career. The Tide went on to defeat NC State 21–0 behind the play of Namath's backup, Steve Sloan. Namath would return sparingly during the rest of the season, with Sloan guiding the offense, and plenty of help from backs Steve Bowman and Les Kelley and receivers Tommy Tolleson, Ray Ogden, David Ray (who also expertly handled placekicking duties), and Ray Perkins.

Despite the injury, Namath still had some remarkable moments, coming off the bench in a tense game at Georgia Tech to throw two touchdown passes in the span of less than two minutes en route to a 24–7 Crimson Tide victory. The bitterness between the two teams was underscored when Bryant wore a helmet on the field during his team's pregame walkthrough. To be sure, the coach was sending a message, but there was also a practical reason, given the depth to which the series had plunged.

"'Yeah, ya'll go ahead and throw your whiskey bottles now,'" Namath recalled Bryant saying. "The few of us that heard this passed Coach Bryant's fighting words back through the line, and I could feel the energy change. We walked around that field behind him, as ready for a game as we'd ever been. Those students were crazy, they would throw all kinds of crap, and man, it was wild. And he had that helmet on, and it loosened us up."

Alabama completed a perfect 10–0 regular season with a 21–14 win over Auburn, highlighted by Ray Ogden's 107-yard kickoff return for a touchdown, a 39-yard fumble scoop and score TD from Steve Bowman, and Namath's 23-yard touchdown pass to Ray Perkins.

With the wire services still releasing their final rankings before the bowl games, the Crimson Tide won its second national championship in four years, finishing first in both the *AP* and *UPI* polls. Next up was a showdown for the ages with Texas.

The 1965 Orange Bowl

It would be the first Orange Bowl game ever played at night, and with it, the first national primetime live broadcast of a college football game. It would also be broadcast in "living color," which was still a relatively new thing in 1965. If that weren't enough to draw attention, it also featured the last two national champions—Alabama and Texas. NBC expected huge television ratings and they got it, with 25 million households tuned in.

It was, in essence, the biggest stage college football had ever seen, and before it was over, the true talent of Bama quarterback Joe Namath would be apparent to everyone who watched the game. Already, word had spread that Namath would be offered a lucrative contract by the American Football League's New York Jets as soon as his college career was done. But no one could have predicted exactly how this one would turn out.

Despite the knee injury that had sidelined Namath for much of his senior season, there was no bigger name among quarterbacks in college football. Notre Dame quarterback John Huarte, for instance, who had won the Heisman Trophy weeks earlier, would end up third on the depth chart behind Namath and Mike Taliaferro at the Jets that fall.

For now, though, there was a lot to be concerned about with Namath. Although he had been able to come back during the season, and had a major impact in the last game of the season against Auburn, he reinjured his knee in a noncontact drill in practice just four days before the Orange Bowl. The betting lines that had originally listed Alabama as a six-point favorite were now closer to even money with the news about Namath's latest injury.

Bama's Steve Sloan, as reporters noted at the time, was an excellent quarterback, but he could not match Joe Namath's skill as a passer. No one could. And Sloan was dealing with a knee injury of his own, suffered in the Auburn game. No matter, Bryant named him the starter after Namath's latest injury. It was anyone's guess as to how either of Alabama's quarterbacks, neither healthy, would be able to handle Texas's fierce defense, led by All-American linebacker Tommy Nobis.

One thing was clear early on in the game: Texas had come to play. In the first quarter, the Longhorns scored first on a 79-yard run by running back Ernie McCoy, the longest Texas scoring touchdown run in four years. That was followed by a bizarre series of Alabama miscues in the second quarter that would lead to Texas scores. The Crimson Tide forced a Texas punt with about 10 minutes remaining in the first half, but an offside penalty negated it. On the next play, Texas scored on a 69-yard touchdown pass and took a 14–0 lead.

Namath, with his knee tightly bound, came off the bench and led the Crimson Tide on a 14-play, 87-yard drive, capped by a 7-yard touchdown pass to Wayne Trimble. Trailing 14–7, the Tide then blocked a Texas field goal try from the 28 yard line. Bama's David Ray picked up the ball and started heading downfield but fumbled it back to Texas when he was tackled. The Longhorns drove 38 yards in six plays to take a 21–7 halftime lead.

"Every time I think about it, that second quarter seems more like one of those 'Our Gang' comedies," Bryant said after the game.

But Alabama regrouped and shut down Texas completely in the second half. The Longhorns never made it past midfield. Meanwhile, Namath and the Tide went to work. Late in the third quarter, he threw the ball on a perfect strike between two defenders to Bama's Ray Perkins in the end zone. New York Jets coach Weeb Ewbank, watching from the press box, was almost giddy with excitement watching Namath, according to *Sports Illustrated*'s coverage of the game. "Fabulous, fabulous, fabulous," he said. "Reminds me of Unitas. He doesn't have to be tutored. He could take a pro team right now."

Next came a 26-yard Alabama field goal from David Ray in the fourth quarter. With Texas's lead now down to 21–17, Namath led Alabama down to the Texas 6-yard line and a chance to take the lead. Three straight handoffs to fullback Steve Bowman moved the ball to within six inches of the Texas goal line.

"Somebody asked me after all the years had passed, 'How come you didn't score?' And I said it wasn't designed to score. It was just designed to go to the 1-yard line and let somebody else score," joked Bowman in 2015. "I did the best I could."

The next play continues to be a source of argument, albeit good-natured, between Alabama and Texas players on the field that night.

On fourth down, Namath tried a quarterback sneak. *Sports Illustrated* described it this way: "He ignored his knee trouble and disappeared in a cascade of white and orange (Texas) jerseys. Eventually Namath could be seen in the end zone, but only after the play was blown dead."

Namath insisted he had scored, and that one official had signaled a touchdown with upraised arms.

"Then was a conference between all the officials, and the linesman who signaled the score backed down," Namath wrote in his autobiography. "Just like that, I was over the goal line but did not score a touchdown. No touchdown."

Though seven minutes remained in the game, Alabama had lost its best chance to win. Namath, who set an Orange Bowl record at the time with 18 completions for 255 yards and two touchdowns in less than three quarters of play, was named the game's most valuable player, despite the 21–17 defeat. Sportswriters described him as a dejected, but noble, warrior leaving the field that night.

The next day, he signed a $427,000 contract to play for the AFL's New York Jets. It was by far the largest pro football contract in history at that time. Four of the Texas players on the field that night would follow Namath to the New York Jets, including George Sauer, who scored for Texas on that 69-yard pass reception in the second quarter. Sauer would later catch eight passes for 133 yards from Namath during the Jets victory over Baltimore in Super Bowl III.

Paul "Bear" Bryant made no excuses for Alabama's loss.

"The way it turned out, it was awful tough to lose," he told *The Tuscaloosa News*. "But if I was coaching Texas, I'd say that was a great goal line stand."

The next year, Bryant and Alabama would be back in the Orange Bowl. And this time, the outcome would be far different.

16

Seeing Orange Again

The Nebraska Cornhuskers sailed through the 1965 football season with an unblemished 10–0 record, a Big Eight Conference title, and a chance to win a national championship in a New Year's night 1966 showdown with No. 4 Alabama in the Orange Bowl.

For the first time ever, the *Associated Press* had decided to wait until after the bowl games before releasing its final college football poll of the season. Alabama, it has to be said, had a lot to do with that decision. The Crimson Tide had been named national champions by both *AP* and *United Press International* in 1964, before losing 21–17 to Texas in the 1965 Orange Bowl. This year, the bowls would have a significant impact on the rankings. And, as it would turn out, that would be just fine with Alabama.

Earlier in the season, it looked like the team would never make it to a major bowl. The Tide lost its 1965 opener by one point to Georgia following a controversial flea-flicker play late in the game, when a Georgia receiver appeared to be down (his knee touching the ground) when he caught the ball, and before he lateralled it to a teammate, who ran it 73 yards for a touchdown.

Although the game in Athens was televised (the only national coast-to-coast football broadcast of the day), there was no instant replay at the time. The touchdown counted, and Georgia followed it up with a successful 2-point conversion to win, 18–17. Less than a month later, Alabama ran into more misfortune in a game with Tennessee in Knoxville. Locked in a 7–7 tie with the Vols, Alabama sophomore quarterback Kenny Stabler, filling in for an injured Steve Sloan, drove the team down to inside Tennessee's 10-yard line. A field goal from David Ray, one of the best placekickers in the nation, would have won it for Alabama. As Ray prepared to run onto the field, Stabler lined the team up and threw the ball out of bounds to stop the clock. The problem, however, was that Stabler lost track of the downs. He had thrown the ball away on fourth down, with six seconds left. There would be no field-goal attempt. The game ended in a tie.

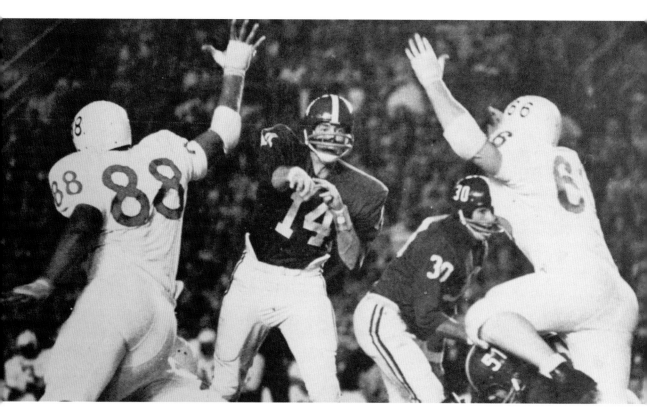

Steve Sloan passing in the 1966 Orange Bowl. (From the *Corolla*, courtesy of the UA Office of Student Media)

Bryant, Stabler later said in his autobiography, was furious.

"I followed Coach Bryant back to the visitors' dressing room at Neyland Stadium," Stabler wrote in *Snake*. "The door was locked and our equipment manager had not arrived yet. Coach Bryant was not going to wait for the key. He brought his right arm back and hit that door with a forearm smash that knocked it, literally, off its hinges."

By the time the players all entered the room, however, Bryant had calmed down to the point where, in an even tone, he blamed himself for the tie, or, as he called it, the "loss."

"I want to apologize for me and my staff not preparing you people well enough to win the game today," Stabler recalled Bryant saying. "It was us, not you, who lost that game. I'm sorry."

"No wonder we all loved that man," Stabler added.

Alabama returned to Tuscaloosa with 3–1–1 record, which may have been acceptable for most teams, but not one this talented, and not at a program as elite as Bryant had established. There would be no other missteps in 1965. Alabama reeled off five consecutive victories, won Bryant's fourth SEC title, and moved back up to No. 4 in the rankings as another primetime appearance in the Orange Bowl approached. No. 1 Michigan State,

No. 2 Arkansas, and No. 3 Nebraska all stood in the Crimson Tide's way of a repeat national championship, but at least the Tide could do something about the Cornhuskers.

Nebraska came into the game leading the nation in rushing, averaging 290 yards per game behind a big offensive line. But Alabama, leaner and faster, and bent on finishing what it had not been able to do against Texas a year earlier, jumped out to a 24–7 halftime lead. The passing combination of Steve Sloan to Ray Perkins proved almost unstoppable, along with rushing from Les Kelley and Steve Bowman.

There was more good news for Alabama in the locker room at halftime. The players already knew that Arkansas had lost in the Cotton Bowl, and now Bryant informed them that Michigan State had just been beaten in the Rose Bowl. The road to a second consecutive national championship was clear. Beat Nebraska and it would be done.

After the Cornhuskers scored on a 49-yard pass to cut the lead to 24–13 in the third quarter, Alabama answered with another scoring drive, this time with Bowman going over from the 1-yard line.

"I'm telling the guys in the huddle before the play, 'Listen, we've already done this once [against Texas],'" Bowman told this writer in 2015. "'We ain't doing it again. I'm not going back through that hell we went through in 1964. It's not gonna happen. We're gonna get this thing in the end zone. That's what we're gonna do.' And that's what we did."

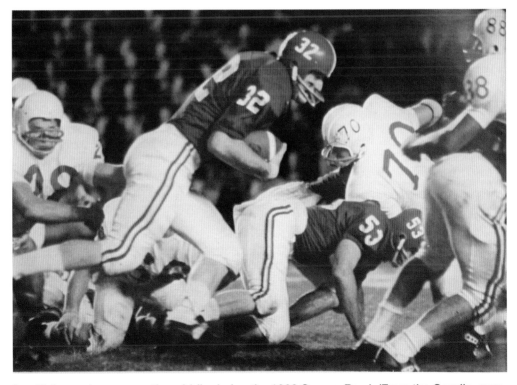

Les Kelley rushes across the middle during the 1966 Orange Bowl. (From the *Corolla*, courtesy of the UA Office of Student Media)

Bowman added another touchdown run in the fourth quarter, and despite a Nebraska rally, Alabama won handily, 39–28. Steve Sloan was named the most valuable player, completing 20 of 28 passes for 296 yards and two touchdowns. His passing performance broke the Orange Bowl record set a year earlier by Namath. Sloan's favorite target, receiver Ray Perkins, caught nine passes for 159 yards, including two for touchdowns. Les Kelley led all rushers with 118 yards and a touchdown, while Bowman rushed for 85 yards and two TDs.

Alabama put up 518 yards of total offense against the previously unbeaten Cornhuskers and held them to 145 rushing yards, less than half their usual average.

By the time Alabama players arrived back in Tuscaloosa the next afternoon, anticipation of the final *Associated Press* college football poll was at a fever pitch. But the players and fans would have to wait into the night. Word finally came to the team in the form of a note posted on the dining room door of Bryant Hall, the new athletic dorm that had been completed less than three years earlier:

January 4, 1966

To squad:

Was notified at 3:32 a.m.

Congratulations national champs.

Paul Bryant

P.S. Let's start today—make it three in a row.

It was official. Alabama had finished No. 1 in the final *AP* rankings—the Crimson Tide's second consecutive national championship and its third in five years.

Said Sam Bailey, the assistant head coach who, *The Tuscaloosa News* reported, had joined Bryant for coffee at four a.m., minutes after the coach broke the news to his team: "I guess this is the nearest thing to a miracle in college athletics that there can be, when you consider all of the things that went into it. Not only did our kids come through like they did, but the others (Michigan State and Arkansas) got beat, too."

The fact that none of the players and coaches had gotten any sleep that night made no difference. Sleep could wait. There was a championship to celebrate.

17

"The Missing Ring"

Paul Bryant was never one to dwell too much on the past. The best coaches never do. There is always the next game, and, as the saying goes, "Don't let last week's loss beat you again by refusing to get over it." And besides, Bryant didn't lose much in his first decade as Alabama's coach.

If anything continued to grate on him, however, it wasn't a loss or a moment in time. It was an entire season—a perfect one in 1966 that should have earned the Crimson Tide a third consecutive national championship. Back-to-back-to-back titles. But it didn't work out that way.

Led by junior quarterback Ken Stabler (whom Bryant later called a "left-handed Namath"), receivers Ray Perkins and Dennis Homan, offensive tackle Cecil Dowdy, defensive tackle Richard Cole, and defensive back Bobby Johns, Alabama won all 11 games, most of them in routs. Only one game was close, an 11–10 come-from-behind victory over Tennessee in the rain in Knoxville. Otherwise, the Tide shut out six opponents, including the last four it faced in the regular season—winning those games over LSU, South Carolina, Southern Miss, and Auburn by a combined 110–0.

And in a rematch with Nebraska, this time in the Sugar Bowl on January 2, 1967, Alabama destroyed the Cornhuskers 34–7.

"I think last year's team was a fine one, but this is one much better," Nebraska coach Bob Devaney said after the game. A year earlier, Alabama had defeated his team 39–28 in the Orange Bowl to win the national title. "The defense is much better and the offense quite a bit better."

Devaney added, when asked: "I'd be crazy to say any ball club is better than them today, I couldn't say anything but that Alabama is No. 1."

Yet, Alabama, which had begun the season ranked No. 1 in the polls, and raced to an 11–0 record, found itself ranked No. 3 in both the *Associated Press* and *United Press*

International final polls, behind Notre Dame and Michigan State, which had famously played to a 10–10 tie late in the season. Worse, it looked like Notre Dame, at least, had actually played "for" the tie, getting the ball back on its own 30-yard line after a punt with 1:24 left in the game and running out the clock from there without ever passing the ball or calling time-out. Michigan State did use its last time-out, hoping to get the ball back, but in the end couldn't do anything but watch the clock tick down to zero as the Fighting Irish did nothing.

"We couldn't believe it," Michigan State's George Webster told *Sports Illustrated*. "When they came up for their first play we kept hollering back and forth, 'Watch the pass, watch the pass.' But they ran. We knew the next one was a pass for sure. But they ran again. We were really stunned. Then it dawned on us. They were settling for the tie."

Wrote *SI*'s Dan Jenkins: "Put the No. 1 team, Notre Dame, on its own 30 yard line with time for at least four passing plays to break the tie. A No. 1 team will try something, won't it, to stay that way? Notre Dame did not. It just let the air out of the ball."

Neither Michigan State nor Notre Dame went to a bowl game, further frustrating Alabama, which had put its undefeated season on the line against Nebraska in the Sugar Bowl. Notre Dame was still refusing to accept bowl bids at that time, and Michigan State was prevented from going to the Rose Bowl by a now-abolished Big 10 Conference rule that said none of its teams could play in that game two years in a row. (The league also wouldn't allow its teams to go to other bowls.)

Bryant expressed his frustration in his 1974 autobiography.

"The 1966 Alabama team was the best I ever had and got done in by the ballot box," he wrote. "We were locked out of the national championship by Notre Dame and Michigan State, who got more attention by playing a 10–10 tie. That's my prejudiced opinion, of course. I said at the time that Notre Dame didn't deserve it because they actually played for a tie in that game, and if you don't at least try to win you don't deserve the championship. I have to admit now that Ara (Parseghian) made the right decision—if he won it (the national championship), which he did, he was right."

Keith Dunnavant, in a book about the 1966 Alabama team called *The Missing Ring*, labeled the pollsters' refusal to rank Alabama No. 1 "the greatest injustice in the history of the national championship selection process."

He accurately noted that in the history of the wire service polls, no preseason No. 1 team (as Alabama was) that went undefeated and untied had ever been denied the title.

There have been many arguments as to why Alabama finished behind Notre Dame and Michigan State. Bryant, for instance, said that after Alabama won two titles in a row, pollsters might have simply been tired of Alabama winning it so much. Today, it would be called "Alabama fatigue," with the Crimson Tide and Nick Saban winning so many

Paul "Bear" Bryant on the cover of *Sports Illustrated* in 1966.

championships that it has become fashionable in many parts of the country to pull against Bama.

But Dunnavant, in *The Missing Ring*, indicates that the racial turmoil in the state of Alabama at the time, with George Wallace's fiery segregation stance and stand in the schoolhouse door back in 1963, the church bombing that killed four young black girls in Birmingham, and the specter of civil rights workers attacked with police dogs and fire houses in Birmingham, had an effect on the college football poll votes in 1966—along with the fact that Alabama's team remained all-white at the time.

Bryant and his program, of course, had nothing to do with attacks on civil rights workers, and in fact, the championship titles Alabama won during those years were a source of positive publicity for the state. Bryant had been talking for some time with black high school coaches about recruiting their athletes. He would later prove to be highly successful recruiting black players, and his fully integrated teams would go on to win three more national championships and six SEC titles in the 1970s. But for now, for whatever reason, the members of the 1966 team would not get national championship rings, despite their unblemished record. The Southeastern Conference championship would have to do.

The 1966 season also capped what amounted to a 1960s dynasty by Bryant and his teams: Alabama teams went 60–5–1 in a six-year run from 1961 through 1966, a remarkable stretch that included three national championships, four SEC titles, two perfect 11–0 seasons, and five bowl victories. The last three of those years, 1964–1966, included a 30–1–1 record that would be unmatched until Bryant's teams in the late 1970s. The 1960s run also included two long winning streaks—a 19-game streak in 1961–62 and a 17-game streak in 1965–66.

18

Snake

It was one of those Saturdays best fit for staying indoors. Because outside was no place to be, unless you happened to enjoy a howling wind, a soaking rain, the threat of tornadoes, and a sky the color of a tattered old shoe. A bad novelist would have described it as a "dark and stormy afternoon."

Gloomy would not only be an appropriate description of the weather, it would also pretty much describe the Alabama football team's chances of winning the Iron Bowl as the fourth quarter got underway in Birmingham's Legion Field on December 2, 1967.

Normally, this would be the place to mention how amazing it was that more than 71,000 fans would subject themselves to such inhospitable conditions, with sustained winds of 20 mph, gusts up to 40, nonending rain, and those tornadoes, which had been reported elsewhere in the state. But who are we kidding? This was Alabama-Auburn. There was no way they would have stayed home. So they grabbed their umbrellas (they were still allowed in stadiums then), ponchos, raincoats, and plastic sheets and headed for the stadium. And here they were, watching a sloppy game in miserable conditions, on a miserable field that had been shredded by a season's worth of college and high school football games and now, with a cold rain pouring down, was a swamp on the edges and a sea of mud and water in the middle.

"Those were the worst field conditions I've ever seen a football game played in," coach Paul "Bear" Bryant said after the game.

It was so bad that Alabama's Kenny "Snake" Stabler, a left-handed gunslinger of a quarterback who would go on to throw for nearly 28,000 yards in a brilliant pro career, only attempted five passes all afternoon. One was intercepted by Auburn, another fell incomplete, and three were caught by Bama receivers for a total of 12 yards. Yes, 12 total yards passing for the *entire* game. Auburn quarterback Lauren Carter fared far better, completing 10 passes for 177 yards, but also throwing a couple of interceptions and despite his

Ken Stabler's 1967 game-winning TD run in the mud against Auburn. (From the *Corolla*, courtesy of the UA Office of Student Media)

sort of miraculous success through the air in an unholy downpour had little to show for it. Twice Auburn had passed up field goal tries in the first half, from the Tide 3- and 7-yard lines, but had finally put some points on the board with a 38-yard field goal in the third quarter. That remained the only score as the clock ticked down under the 12-minute mark in the fourth quarter.

Long before Stabler found himself mired in the mud, his team going nowhere that afternoon, with only two first downs in more than three quarters of play, he had earned a reputation for dodging, twisting, turning, and scrambling his way around and through an opponent's defense. Such daring feats had been common back in his junior high and high school playing days in Foley, Alabama. "In the eighth or ninth grade, he'd run 200 yards to score from 20 yards out," Denzil Hollis, Stabler's junior high coach told *Sports Illustrated* in 1977.

Stabler's slithering his way to touchdowns led Hollis and others to begin referring to him as "Snake," and it was a nickname that would stick—through a 29–1 record as the starting quarterback at Foley High School, through an extraordinary run at Alabama, and on to a legendary career with the Oakland Raiders, where he won the NFL's Most Valuable Player award in 1976 and a masterful 32–14 Super Bowl XI victory over Minnesota on January 9, 1977.

But here, back in the mud of Legion Field in 1967, it was do-or-die time for the Alabama offense on a third down at Auburn's 47 yard line. Stabler took a snap from center, rolled on an option play to his right, and, with his trailing halfback covered by Auburn's smothering defense, decided to keep the ball and turn it up field. Bama receiver Dennis Homan laid down a perfect block, taking out Auburn defender Buddy McClinton, and Stabler was free down the sideline, keeping his footing in the mud and water and racing 47 yards to the end zone. He carried an Auburn defender on his back the final three yards. It was one of the most spectacular touchdowns in Crimson Tide history and instantly became known as "the run in the mud."

The clock stood at 11:29 left in the fourth quarter when Stabler scored, and after a successful extra point, Alabama took a 7–3 lead that it would never give up.

"And afterward, Coach Bryant came to me and said, 'Son, I am as proud of you as anybody who's ever been here. You've done a great job for me on and off the field,'" Stabler said in his 1986 autobiography, *Snake*.

The praise from Bryant was significant because, like he had once done with Joe Namath, the coach had earlier suspended Stabler for rules violations. In Stabler's case, after being sidelined by a knee injury in spring practice, he had begun skipping classes, taken to driving back and forth to Mobile to visit a girlfriend (and collecting a stack of speeding tickets in the process), and missing team meetings. Bryant had allowed him back on the team for fall practice but forced him to start at the bottom of the depth chart. By the time Alabama opened the 1967 season against Florida State, Stabler had worked his way back up, though he didn't start. No matter, Bryant sent him in on Alabama's second offensive series, and the starting job was his again for good. The Auburn victory in the mud, as it turned out, would be the highlight of an 8–2–1 season that included a 20–16 upset loss to Texas A&M in the Cotton Bowl. The Aggies were coached by Gene Stallings, who had played for Bryant at A&M back in the 1950s and had served with him as an assistant coach in Bryant's first years at Alabama. No one could have known it then, but Stallings would lead Alabama to a national championship in 1992—twenty-five years after defeating his old coach and the Tide in the Cotton Bowl.

19

Breaking the Color Barrier

Though Alabama's outstanding football teams under Bear Bryant in the 1960s were the pride of the state and gained countless fans nationally, there was no getting around the fact that the program remained segregated throughout the decade. But change was coming.

For Bryant, the fact that the Crimson Tide overcame considerable resistance within the state to playing integrated teams was no small victory in the move toward equality on and off the playing field.

"When folks are ignorant, you don't condemn them, you teach 'em," Bryant said in his autobiography. "We began to break down resistance in Alabama when we played Penn State in the Liberty Bowl in 1959, and then Oklahoma and Nebraska in the Orange Bowl later on." Those teams were all integrated.

Bryant was not exaggerating about the resistance. For instance, author and filmmaker Keith Dunnavant's 2013 documentary, *Three Days at Foster: How Integration Turned the Tide*, included a telegram sent to Bryant on December 7, 1959, from Citizens Council of West Alabama. It read: "We strongly oppose our boys playing an integrated team. We hope this has been taken care of. The Tide belongs to all Alabama, and Alabamians favor continued segregation."

That note and others like it, of course, did not speak, as they claimed, for "all" Alabamians, and Bryant understood that. Black residents and players were just as much a part of Alabama as white residents, and the coach made plans to not only play integrated teams, but to integrate his own. Five black players walked on at Alabama in the spring of 1967, and though, like many walk-ons, they didn't ultimately make the team that fall, the future was clear: Bryant made plans to integrate Alabama's football team, and once he did, the black athletes who played for him said the coach tolerated no racism in his program.

"Coach Bryant was like my second father," John Mitchell, assistant head coach of the

Pittsburgh Steelers, said in a Showtime documentary, *Against the Tide*. "I wouldn't be here today if it was not for him."

Mitchell, a junior college transfer in 1971, became the first African-American player to enter a game for Alabama. But the first to sign to play for the Tide and receive a scholarship was Wilbur Jackson in December 1969. NCAA rules still prohibited freshmen from playing for the varsity, so when the integrated USC Trojans came to Birmingham to play Alabama in the opener of the 1970 season, Jackson was watching in the stands.

USC crushed Alabama 42–21, with all six of the Trojans' touchdowns scored by black players. Most notably, the Trojans' sophomore running back, Sam "Bam" Cunningham, playing in his first varsity game, ripped through Alabama's defense, gaining 135 yards, and two touchdowns on just 12 carries. And it could have been worse. USC coach John McKay, a close friend of Bryant's, began substituting in the third quarter.

"Coach McKay saw what was happening and he pulled the dogs off," former Alabama assistant coach Pat Dye (later head coach at Auburn) said in *Against the Tide*. "They could have beat us a hundred to nothing."

Although Alabama had already integrated the program by signing Jackson, the game was nevertheless credited with breaking down any remaining resistance among Alabama fans to the integration of the football team.

"An Alabama fan, a week or so later, when I stopped by to get some gas in Tuscaloosa, came over and started talking about the game, and he says, 'We've got to have some of those players.' And I thought, 'OK, the light's gone on here,'" said Scott Hunter, who was the Bama quarterback the night of the USC game.

A few myths about the game lingered for decades, including one in which Bryant supposedly brought USC's Cunningham into the Tide dressing room after the game, asked him to stand on a chair, and told his players, "Fellows, this is what a football player looks like."

But it never happened.

"Coach Bryant would never have brought a player in and embarrassed us or the team," Hunter said in *Against the Tide*. "He never brought a football player into our locker room and said this is what a football player looks like. That didn't happen."

Instead, Cunningham told the documentary filmmakers that Bryant met him in the hallway between the two locker rooms and "congratulated me."

"It kind of got started that I got taken into the other locker room," Cunningham added. "But I didn't go into their locker room. I didn't shake any of their guys' hands, and I didn't get put up on a pedestal. Nothing like that, but that just kind of surfaced and kept rolling for thirty-something years."

Bryant did, however, go into USC's locker room.

"After the game, coach Bryant came into the locker room, stood on top of a bench in front of the lockers, and congratulated the guys on their win, and said, 'You played a great game' and so on and so forth," said USC assistant coach Dave Levy. "And I thought that showed a lot of class."

A year later, Alabama would meet USC again, this time in the Los Angeles Coliseum. The outcome would be much different. And John Mitchell, who joined Alabama as a community college transfer before the 1971 season, would have a lot to do with the outcome. Alabama was no longer a segregated team, and the team, its coaches, fans, and the state of Alabama would be all the better for it.

Part Three

20

A Secret Offense and Sweet Revenge

When Alabama players arrived for fall camp in 1971, Bryant informed them he was scrapping the pro-set offense the Crimson Tide had run for years and would, instead, run the wishbone, a triple-option rushing attack used successfully by Texas and Oklahoma. Practices were closed, and players were told to keep quiet. When the SEC "Skywriters" tour of sports reporters flew into town for an annual preseason visit, Bryant had the team switch back to the pro-set for that one afternoon to protect the best-kept secret in college football.

So on Friday, September 10, 1971, when Alabama took the field for a rematch with Southern California, the Trojans were caught completely unaware.

"We had exchanged spring practice films. They were running roughly the same offense they ran in 1970," USC assistant coach Dave Levy said in *Against the Tide*, a Showtime documentary. "And at game time, they show up and run a wishbone. I would call that the greatest snooker job of all time."

Led by quarterback Terry Davis, running back Johnny Musso, big offensive lineman John Hannah, and defenders Robin Parkhouse, Steve Higginbotham, and John Mitchell, the Crimson Tide raced out to a 17–0 lead and held on, winning it 17–10 before a stunned crowd of 68,000 at the Los Angeles Coliseum. Almost lost in the press coverage over the victory and the success of the new wishbone offense was the fact that Mitchell, a junior college transfer, had become the first African-American player to take the field with the Crimson Tide. And as Bryant would point out, they had USC's John McKay to thank for that.

In the off-season, McKay had let it slip to Bryant that the Trojans were recruiting an outstanding defensive end from Mobile, Alabama. The player, Mitchell, was attending junior college in Arizona. Bryant, even without seeing film of Mitchell's playing days in high school or junior college, immediately recruited him with the help of contacts in Mobile that included Bama's recently graduated former quarterback, Scott Hunter. Mitchell had a major impact on the game defensively for Alabama that night in Los Angeles and would go on to become the Crimson Tide's first black All-American and captain.

Many of the same USC players who had routed Alabama a year earlier in Birmingham were still on the team that night. For the Crimson Tide, it was sweet revenge, and the beginning of another resurgence in the program. Significantly, it was also Bryant's 200th career win.

The Tide's wishbone broke a flurry of rushing records en route to an 11–1 season and a tenth SEC championship for the program, five of them with Bryant as coach. The highlight, aside from the USC game, was a 31–7 thrashing of then-undefeated Auburn, led by Heisman Trophy winner Pat Sullivan. But Alabama ran into a brick wall of its own in the Orange Bowl, suffering an uncharacteristic 38–7 blowout loss to the undefeated, national champion Cornhuskers. Many consider that 1971 Cornhusker team to be one of the most dominant in college football history.

21

A Perfect Season and a Showdown with Notre Dame

By the time Alabama opened its 1973 season against California at Birmingham's Legion Field, the Crimson Tide's wishbone offense had been firmly established as one of the best in the nation, with two years of fine-tuning.

So Cal got the full brunt of it on September 15, when Alabama emptied its bench in a 66–0 rout over the Bears. The Tide's wishbone offense churned up a school record 667 yards of total offense.

The next week, things got a bit tougher when Bryant took his team to Lexington to play Kentucky for the first time since he had been head coach there back in 1953. The Tide fell behind 14–0 before scoring 28 unanswered points in the second half, including a 100-yard kickoff return for a touchdown from Willie Shelby to open the third quarter. The 28–14 Bama victory would mark the first of only two times all season that teams would come within two touchdowns of Alabama.

The offensive onslaught Bama had unleashed on Cal in the opening game would pale in comparison to the Tide's 77–6 slaughter of Virginia Tech on October 27. Alabama shattered the NCAA single-game rushing record with 743 yards and also broke the SEC's total offense mark with 828 overall yards. It could have been even worse. Alabama led Virginia Tech 70–6 after three quarters and played everyone with a crimson jersey in an effort to keep the scoring down.

The offense led by quarterback Gary Rutledge, running backs Wilbur Jackson and James Taylor, center Sylvester Croom, wide receiver Wayne Wheeler, and backup QB Richard Todd, among others, was almost unstoppable. The defense, with Woodrow Lowe, Mike Washington, John Croyle, and Mike DuBose, among others, could bend at times but never broke.

The team sailed through the rest of the season, with the offense making one spectacular play after another. Among them: two highlight-reel touchdowns in a 42–21 victory over rival Tennessee that included an opening play 80-yard pass from Gary Rutledge to Wayne Wheeler and an 80-yard run from Wilbur Jackson. There were many others, as well, such as a 77-yard touchdown strike from Rutledge to Wheeler en route to a 21–7 victory over LSU in Baton Rouge.

Alabama ended the regular season with a 35–0 rout of Auburn in the Iron Bowl, avenging a bizarre 17–16 upset loss a year earlier in which the Tigers had won on two nearly identical scoop-and-score blocked Bama punts.

The Tide finished No. 1 in *United Press International*'s final coaches poll of the season, released before the bowl games. It was the fourth national title for Bryant at Alabama. The team also won the program's 12th SEC championship, seven of them with Bryant as coach.

Still, there was one huge game left, a showdown with Notre Dame in the Sugar Bowl. Both teams were unbeaten, with Alabama ranked No. 1 in both the *Associated Press* and *UPI* polls, and Notre Dame No. 3 in *AP* and No. 4 in *UPI*. For Alabama, it was a chance to make a statement after being denied the national championship in 1966 when Notre Dame finished No. 1, even though they had not accepted a bowl invitation and had famously played to a 10–10 tie with Michigan State in the regular season.

The Sugar Bowl, scheduled for New Year's Eve at New Orleans' Tulane Stadium, was the first-ever meeting between the Crimson Tide and the Fighting Irish, and it was as eagerly anticipated as any game in college football history. It more than lived up to the billing—turning out to be a nail-biter for fans of both teams. There were repeated lead changes, big plays, and finally a last series that would decide the game late in the fourth quarter. Trailing 24–23, Alabama had Notre Dame backed up with a third down on their own 3-yard line, and just over two minutes left in the game. One stop and the Irish would have to punt from their own end zone, giving Alabama the ball with excellent field position for a short drive and a game-winning field goal. But it didn't work out that way.

Notre Dame quarterback Tom Clements took the snap, dropped back into the end zone, and completed a 35-yard pass down the sideline for a first down. Alabama defenders were clearly not expecting such a long throw from the end zone. The Irish were able to run out the clock from there. It was a crushing defeat for Alabama, and it won the *AP* national championship for Notre Dame.

Bryant, however, had weathered losses before and brought his teams back to even greater heights. He would do it again later in the 1970s. Reflecting back on the game with Notre Dame, he wrote in his autobiography: "I don't really consider it a loss, we just ran out of time."

22

The 1970s: Decade of Dominance

Alabama's 11–1 seasons in 1971 and 1973 were the beginning of one of the most dominant decades any team ever had in college football—and would not be matched until Nick Saban took over as head coach of the Crimson Tide in the twenty-first century. From 1971 through 1979, Bryant's Alabama teams went 97–13, including three national championships, eight SEC titles, and seven 11-win seasons.

Add that to three national titles and five SEC championships Bryant's teams had already won in the 1960s, and it all became part of a legacy for the ages.

"I don't think there's any question that there's probably only a few people in college athletics history that have had as great an impact. Maybe John Wooden at UCLA," Nick Saban said on what would have been Bryant's 100th birthday in 2013. "I think that as a coach, since I've been here, you can't have enough respect for the number of players who come back and talk about Coach Bryant, the influence and impact that he had on their life, and how he affected people in a really positive way, which is part of what we all try to do as coaches. I have probably as much respect for that part of what he did as anything."

Despite Bryant's enormous success, his teams continued to struggle against Notre Dame, not only losing the 1973 Sugar Bowl by one point, but also a two-point loss to the Irish in the Orange Bowl in 1975, and a three-point loss to them in the 1976 regular season, after which Bryant said: "It's getting worse with age. One, two, and three points. I doubt that I'll make it to the four-pointer."

He did, however, make it to the fourth game, held at Birmingham's Legion Field in 1980. His team lost that one, too, 7–0. It would be up to later Alabama teams following Bryant's era to handle Notre Dame, first winning against the Irish in a game at Birmingham's Legion Field in 1986. And following the 2012 season, Nick Saban and the Crimson

Paul Bryant. (From the *Corolla*, courtesy of the UA Office of Student Media)

Tide routed an undefeated Notre Dame team 42–14 in the 2013 BCS national championship game in Miami.

But no team or coach during Bryant's era could fully match his ability to keep a team in contention for championships over a couple of decades. For Bryant, his last two national championships would come in 1978 and 1979. And another season, in 1977, which featured two of the best offensive players to ever suit up in crimson and white—All-Americans Ozzie Newsome at receiver and Johnny Davis at fullback—could just as well have ended in a national title. The Crimson Tide went 11–1 that year, losing only in a close away game at Nebraska early in the season. But Alabama rebounded to defeat Southern California in Los Angeles and went unbeaten through a tough SEC schedule. The Tide ended the season with a 35–6 blowout win over Ohio State in the Sugar Bowl. It was the first-ever meeting between those two great programs and their larger-than-life coaches, Bryant and Woody Hayes.

Alabama had been ranked No. 3 going into the bowls, behind No. 1 Texas and No. 2 Oklahoma. Both of those teams lost their bowl games, but instead of moving up to No. 1, the Crimson Tide was leap-frogged in both polls by No. 5 Notre Dame, the team that had defeated Texas in a 38–10 blowout in the Cotton Bowl.

"Naturally, I'm disappointed for our players and our staff because they did an outstanding job this year," Bryant said. "We came so far this year against one of the toughest schedules in the country. But Notre Dame has our congratulations."

Alabama quarterback Jeff Rutledge, whose older brother Gary had led the team's offense just four years earlier, expressed his frustration over the voting.

"It's just not fair," he said. "We need a playoff system if that's the way they are picked. We should be No. 1 if it's done mathematically. When the No. 1 and No. 2 teams get beat, the third-ranked team should be No. 1. It's as simple as that."

Rutledge's angst over voters deciding the outcome would be echoed well into the twenty-first century by other players and other teams who believed that major college football should have a playoff to determine its champion. Just such a playoff would begin with the 2014 season, though with only four teams, as chosen by a select committee comprised primarily of former coaches, players, and athletic directors. Nevertheless, it would be a major improvement over the system college football teams faced in the twentieth century and give far more order to the way the national championship is decided.

And Alabama would figure prominently in the new system.

23

"You better pass."

Alabama began the 1978 season with three high-powered nonconference opponents—tenth ranked Nebraska, eleventh-ranked Missouri, and seventh-ranked Southern California. It was as tough an opening act as any team in the nation faced, and when it was done, the Tide owned a 2–1 record, following a 20–3 win over the Cornhuskers, a 38–20 victory at Mizzou, and a 28–14 loss to Southern California at Birmingham's Legion Field.

From there, however, the Crimson Tide reeled off eight consecutive victories, including another high profile nonconference win in Seattle over the Washington Huskies and a steady march through a challenging SEC schedule. The Tide, which had been the *Associated Press*'s preseason No. 1 team and dropped to as low as No. 8 after the USC loss, was back in the hunt—ranked No. 2 at the end of the season.

Next, they would face unbeaten, top-ranked Penn State in the Sugar Bowl in a meeting of the nation's No. 1 and No. 2 teams.

A great part of Alabama's success on offense was attributable to two teammates who, like so many players in the program down through the years, had once been competitors in high school. But quarterback Jeff Rutledge and running back Tony Nathan had a high school rivalry experience that stands out. In 1974, Rutledge was quarterback for the two-time defending Alabama state 4A champion Banks High School Jets in Birmingham, and Nathan was the star running back for the cross-town rival Woodlawn High Colonels. The two teams, both unbeaten, met on a November night in 1974 at Birmingham's Legion Field in a game that drew 42,000 people, the largest crowd ever seen at a high school game in the state of Alabama. Only one could advance to the state playoffs—and the hoopla surrounding the game centered on Rutledge and Nathan. Both delivered: Rutledge completed nine of ten passes for 188 yards and a touchdown en route to an 18–7 victory over Woodlawn. Banks' defense gave Nathan fits all night, but the talented running back, who would later go on to play for nine seasons with the NFL's Miami Dolphins (including two Super Bowls), rushed 31 times for 112 yards, including a 13-yard touchdown run.

The game became a focal point in an inspiring 2015 film, *Woodlawn*, about the desegregation of Woodlawn High and a spiritual awakening among the team.

Now, getting ready to face Penn State, both Nathan and Rutledge would have plenty of help from other Alabama offensive standouts that included Major Ogilvie, Billy Jackson, Steve Whitman, Bruce Bolton, Buddy Aydelette, Mike Brock, Keith Pugh, Lou Ikner, and Rick Neal. The Crimson Tide also featured one of the nation's best defenses, led by Marty Lyons, Barry Krauss, Rich Wingo, Wayne Hamilton, David Hannah, Murray Legg, Don McNeal, E. J. Junior, Warren Lyles, Allen Crumbly, and Rickey Gilliland, among others.

But for all its buildup, the 1979 Sugar Bowl between two outstanding teams would come down to what became known simply as the "Goal Line Stand." With Alabama leading 14–7 midway through the fourth quarter, Penn State recovered a fumble at the Tide's 19-yard line. An 11-yard run afterward gave the Nittany Lions a first down and goal to go at the Tide's 8-yard line. Another run moved the ball to the 6, and on second down from there, Penn State quarterback Chuck Fusina connected with split end Scott Fitzkee on a short pass. It looked like it would be a sure touchdown, given the angle Fitzkee had heading toward the right corner of the end zone. That is, until Alabama's Don McNeal met Fitzkee at the 1-yard line and drove him out of bounds. Though some other heroics were about to follow for Alabama's team, they wouldn't have been possible without McNeal's outstanding effort to keep Penn State from scoring on second down.

Next, with a third and goal at the 1-yard line, Fusina handed the ball off to running back Matt Suhey, who tried to dive over the Tide's line but got nowhere. In the seconds after the play, with the New Orleans Superdome crowd of nearly 77,000 nearly raising the roof in an electric, tense atmosphere, Fusina walked over to take a look at where the ball was placed.

A brief conversation between Fusina and Alabama's Marty Lyons in that moment has since become part of Crimson Tide legend. As the two opposing players who had gotten to know and respect each other at awards events looked at the ball just 10 inches from the goal line, Lyons told Fusina: "You better pass."

Instead, Penn State lined up on fourth down and once again tried a dive play, this time with tailback Mike Guman leaping toward the Alabama line. The Crimson Tide's Barry Krauss met him at the top of the dive and, with the help of Rich Wingo, Murray Legg, and others, stopped Guman cold. Although there were still more than six minutes left, the game was essentially over. Penn State's 19-game winning streak had come to an end. But Alabama's own streak, now at nine games, was nowhere near finished.

After the game, Alabama was chosen national champions by the *Associated Press*, the National Football Foundation, and the Football Writers' Association, among other selectors. The *UPI* coaches poll selected 10–1 USC as the top-ranked team.

For Bryant, it was his fifth national championship at Alabama. But he was not done. The next year would bring an undefeated season and a consensus national title.

Part Three

24

Perfection

The 1979 version of the Crimson Tide was without a significant number of contributors to the national championship team the previous season, but it was nevertheless loaded with talent. Returning were first-team All-Americans Don McNeal at defensive back and center Dwight Stephenson, and they were joined by standouts in the offensive backfield like Major Ogilvie and Steve Whitman, a stout offensive line, and a strong core of defenders that included E. J. Junior and Byron Braggs, to form the basis of a truly monumental season.

The 1978 team had returned Alabama to the top of the college football world, but the 1979 Crimson Tide would go even further—completing a perfect 12–0 season, which would not only break an Alabama record for single-season victories, but would also leave no doubt as to who the national champion was in the sport. There would be no split title between the wire services this season.

With quarterback Steadman Shealy now directing the high-powered wishbone offense, the Tide opened the season with a 30–6 victory over Georgia Tech in Atlanta, gaining more than 300 yards rushing in the process. Next came a 45–0 blowout over Baylor at Birmingham's Legion Field, then a 66–3 romp over Vanderbilt in Nashville, where 14 different Alabama runners touched the ball as Bryant emptied the bench in a not-so-successful effort to keep the score down. Then it was on to a 38–0 shutout at home in what by now had become Bryant-Denny Stadium. It seemed no opponent could stop the best rushing offense in the country. And when needed, Shealy and his backup Don Jacobs could easily pass from the triple option, as well. The following week, Florida got the full brunt of that offensive onslaught, and a swarming defense with it. The Tide shut out the Gators 40–0 in Gainesville, totaling 454 total yards to just 66 for Florida, and 22 first downs to just three for the Gators.

Florida players offered no excuses after the game, saying simply they had played the best team in America.

"There's no shame in losing to the University of Alabama," said the Gators' Cris Collinsworth. "They're the No. 1 team in the country. I'll be very, very surprised if they don't repeat the national championship. What couldn't impress you about Alabama? I got a kick out of playing against them."

Collinsworth, who knew a great football team when he played one, would be prophetic, but that didn't change the fact that the following week, Alabama opened its annual game against Tennessee looking like a far different team. The Tide fell behind the Vols 17–0 before rallying to win it 27–17 in Birmingham. It was Alabama's ninth consecutive victory over Tennessee.

Next came a 31–7 victory over Virginia Tech, followed by a 24–7 win over Mississippi State and then a 3–0 escape in the rain against LSU in Baton Rouge, although the Tigers had gotten the worst end of it—crossing midfield only once the entire game. From there, the Tide put on a 30–0 clinic in Tuscaloosa against former Bryant assistant coach Howard Schnellenberger and his Miami Hurricane team—which featured future Pro Hall of Famer Jim Kelly at quarterback. Alabama ended the regular season with a hard-fought 28–17 victory over Auburn, the Tide's seventh consecutive victory over the Tigers.

Finally, in contrast to the nail-biting fourth quarter "Goal Line Stand" victory a year earlier against Penn State, Alabama dispatched Arkansas 24–9 in the New Year's Day 1980 Sugar Bowl. The Crimson Tide was voted No. 1 in both the *Associated Press* and *United Press International* final polls—winning a consensus national title and leaving a legacy as the team of the decade in the 1970s. It had been a remarkable run.

With the Sugar Bowl victory, Alabama was now on a 21-game winning streak that it would stretch to 28 before an upset loss to Mississippi State in 1980. Paul Bryant had proven that his teams could change with the times, and win in any decade.

25

An Iron Bowl for the Ages

Way back in 1890, two years before The University of Alabama ever fielded a football team, Amos Alonzo Stagg began a head coaching career that would span 57 seasons. As an end at Yale, Stagg was selected to the first-ever College Football All-America team in 1889, and a year later he coached his first game.

All told, his teams went 314–199–35 through the better part of six decades, establishing a record for victories that seemed untouchable following his last season as head coach—at Pacific University—in 1946. But three decades afterward, Alabama sports information director Charley Thornton noticed an interesting statistic: Paul Bryant, prior to the 1978 season, was just 42 victories away from matching Stagg's 314 mark.

Though Bryant had never dwelled on the record, it seemed a perfect way to counteract anti-Alabama recruiting methods in which opposing coaches were telling high school players that Bryant would retire soon.

As author Tommy Ford recalled in *The University of Alabama Football Vault,* Bryant told a meeting of the Birmingham Quarterback Club: "If anybody's going to break the record, it might as well be me."

By the beginning of the 1981 season, Bryant was just nine wins away. That team, led by quarterback Walter Lewis, was determined to shatter the record for him. A thrilling 31–16 road victory over No. 5-ranked Penn State in front of more than 85,000 Nittany Lion fans in Happy Valley on November 14 pulled Bryant into a tie with Stagg at 314 career wins. Now all that remained was one victory, and, fittingly, the next opportunity was an Iron Bowl showdown with Auburn at Birmingham's Legion Field, the site of so many landmark battles in the past.

The Crimson Tide, playing as hard for a coach as any team had ever done, came from behind to defeat Auburn 28–17, giving Bryant a record-breaking 315th college football career victory. In defeat, Auburn coach Pat Dye, who had been an assistant to Bryant at Alabama from 1965 through 1973, called his old boss "the greatest in history."

Bryant praised both his players and Auburn's team for the hard-fought contest and then allowed himself a moment to reflect on his career. "I'm thankful to the good Lord for the many wonderful people at Maryland, Kentucky, Texas A&M, and here," he said.

Breaking the record "hasn't set in yet," he said. "I feel like I ought to go back and check the scoreboard to make sure we won."

Alabama's 1981 team would go on to lose a close game to Texas in the Cotton Bowl on January 1, finishing with a 9–2–1 record. But the imperfect season hardly seemed to matter. It was the nine wins that counted. The following year, 1982, would be Bryant's last. An epic era in college football was coming to an end.

26

Death of an Icon

Paul William "Bear" Bryant died of a heart attack in the early afternoon of January 26, 1983, less than a month after he had coached his last game at Alabama. His death not only jolted the entire state, it also shocked the nation. Bryant had been larger than life, a tall, imposing, forceful leader who, at 69, had reached every goal possible in his profession but was still gone too soon. There was no bigger name in college football, and Bryant had also achieved the sort of celebrity status nationally that few coaches in any sport have ever been afforded.

The outpouring of grief was almost unbearable for Alabama fans, and so, too, for countless other Americans who had never been associated with the program and had never even attended an Alabama game. Not since Knute Rockne's death back in 1931 had anyone ever seen such a national outpouring of heartfelt sadness and reverence for a coach.

It seemed even more tragic that Bryant, who had announced his retirement back on December 15, 1982, two weeks before he coached his last game—a 21–15 victory over UCLA in the Liberty Bowl—would not live long enough to finally enjoy a life without the stresses of a big-time football program. He had once told *Sports Illustrated*'s John Underwood that "I'd croak in a week" if he ever just gave up coaching. It was a joke then, but now it had the ring of truth to it.

It was the end of the most successful run ever in college football. With the Liberty Bowl win, Bryant's final record stood at 323–85–17 (a .780 winning percentage) over a 37-year head coaching career. That included a 232–46–9 run in 25 years at Alabama—an .824 winning percentage that was unheard of for such a long tenure. It included six national championships, 13 SEC titles, and 24 consecutive bowl appearances under his watch.

"Today we Americans lost a hero who always seemed larger than life," said President Ronald Reagan. "Paul 'Bear' Bryant won more college football games than any other coach in history, and he made legends out of ordinary people. Only four weeks ago, we held our breath, then cheered, when the 'Bear' notched his final victory in a game, fittingly, the Liberty Bowl. He was a hard, but loved taskmaster. Patriotic to the core, devoted to his players, and inspired by a winning spirit that would not quit, Bear Bryant gave his country the gift of a life unsurpassed. In making the impossible seem easy, he lived what he strived to be."

Two days after his death, Bryant's funeral was held in Tuscaloosa's First United Methodist Church, with eight players on his final team serving as pallbearers. Tens of thousands of mourners descended on Tuscaloosa, and police estimated that at least 250,000 people jammed roadsides and overpasses along US Interstate 20/59 to witness the three-mile-long funeral procession as it made its way 55 miles, from Tuscaloosa to Bryant's gravesite in Birmingham's Elmwood Cemetery.

"It was the most amazing sight I've ever seen," said USC's former head coach John McKay, one of Bryant's closest friends in coaching. "It was like a presidential funeral procession. No coach in America could have gotten that. No coach but him. But then he wasn't just a coach. He was *the* coach."

Bear Bryant's statue outside Bryant-Denny Stadium. (Photo by Mark Mayfield)

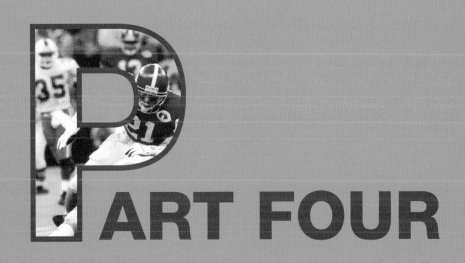

PART FOUR

GLIMPSES OF PAST GLORY: ALABAMA IN THE POST-BRYANT ERA

27

Miracle Comebacks

Paul "Bear" Bryant would prove a hard act to follow. The job first went to Ray Perkins, a wide receiver who had played with both Joe Namath and Ken Stabler and was named a first-team All-American on Bryant's undefeated 1966 team. Perkins had gone on to play for the Baltimore Colts and later became head coach of the New York Giants. Perkins left the Giants—one of the most sought-after coaching jobs in the NFL—to accept Alabama's offer to succeed his old coach.

His four-year record at Alabama was 32–15–1 and included some big wins over Ohio State, Southern California, and most notably the program's first-ever victory over Notre Dame—a 28–10 win in Birmingham notable especially for a thundering sack that Bama All-American linebacker Cornelius Bennett administered to Irish quarterback Steve Beuerlein.

But Perkins also rankled Crimson Tide fans by removing Bryant's legendary tower from the practice field, replacing Alabama's longtime, popular football radio broadcaster John Forney with a young play-by-play announcer from Nashville, and replacing most of Bryant's assistants with his own staff—a move that would seem entirely normal, given any other coaching change that didn't involve succeeding a legend like Bryant.

"One of the things I learned from him [Bryant] as far as coaching is concerned was 'Do it your way,'" Perkins told this author during an interview for *USA Today* back in 1986. "I don't coach from a tower. Coach Bryant did. So I really can't understand the criticism. As far as the coaching staff, I've always believed it's better for all involved that when a coach receives a new head coaching position anywhere, there should be total change."

Perkins resigned as Alabama's coach, following a 10–3 season in 1986, to accept the head coaching job with the Tampa Bay Buccaneers. His decision cut short what might have been a successful long-term tenure in Tuscaloosa. Looking back on those brief four years, two come-from-behind victories in the final seconds especially stand out—both in

1985. The first came in the opening game with Georgia in Athens. Alabama's offense had the ball trailing 16–13 with no time-outs, just 50 seconds left in the game, and 71 yards in front of them to the end zone. Led by quarterback Mike Shula, the Tide drove the length of the field and scored on Shula's 18-yard strike across the middle to Al Bell. Van Tiffin added an extra point, and Alabama won it 20–16.

The Crimson Tide found itself in a similar position on November 30, 1985, in the Iron Bowl in Birmingham. Trailing Auburn 23–22 with just 57 seconds remaining, Shula and the Tide offense stood 80 yards away from the end zone. An incomplete pass and then an 8-yard sack made matters even worse—not to mention there were now just 37 seconds left in the game, with Bama on its own 12-yard line, 88 yards away.

On third and 18, Shula completed a perfect 14-yard strike to halfback Gene Jelks, who lunged out of bounds to stop the clock. It was now fourth and four. Alabama ran a reverse, with Al Bell taking a handoff deep in the backfield and rushing around the left end and down the sideline for 20 yards and a first down at the Tide 46. An incomplete pass came next. On second down, and with no time-outs, Shula dropped back in the pocket,

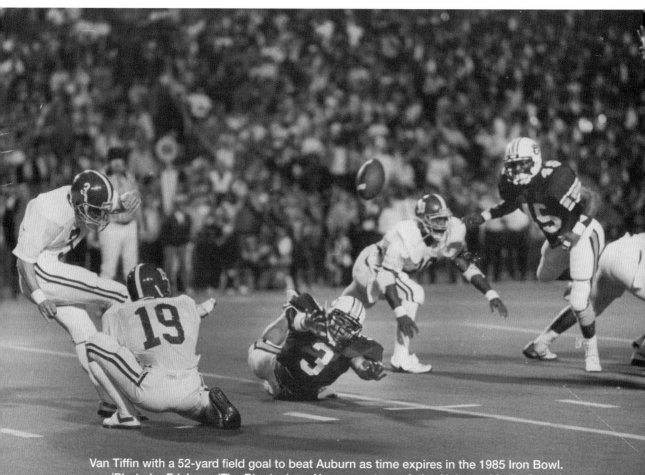

Van Tiffin with a 52-yard field goal to beat Auburn as time expires in the 1985 Iron Bowl. (Photo by Ed Jones/*The Birmingham News*, courtesy of the Alabama Media Group)

hesitating with his receivers covered, then threw to Greg Richardson, who caught the ball in the middle of the field and raced toward the sideline, carrying an Auburn defender with him the final three or four yards to get out of bounds and stop the clock.

There were six seconds left in the game. Bama placekicker Van Tiffin ran onto the field and, with the clock winding down toward zero, kicked a 52-yard field goal through the middle of the uprights, giving Alabama a thrilling 25–23 victory.

"It was almost like an out-of-body experience," Tiffin said later.

Simply known as "The Kick," the sensational finish to one of the greatest Iron Bowl games ever is a moment Crimson Tide fans will never forget.

Part Four

28

Gene Stallings and the Game That Changed College Football

It was December 5, 1992, and it was the start of something big, not only for Alabama and Florida, who were about to battle at Birmingham's Legion Field, but also a monumental occasion for the Southeastern Conference and college football in general.

No major conference had decided its football champion in a postseason game. Until now. Led by commissioner Roy Kramer, the SEC expanded its membership from 10 to 12, adding South Carolina and Arkansas, divided into East and West divisions, and for the first time in its history created a postseason game that would decide its champion.

And this would be the first one. For Alabama, which had struggled for years to repeat the runaway success of the Paul Bryant era, the magic was back. The Crimson Tide, using a balanced offense and a stifling defense, was 11–0 and ranked No. 2 in the nation. In any other year, the team would already have punched its ticket to the Sugar Bowl to play the unbeaten defending national champion Miami Hurricanes. But not so this year. There was this extra game against the East division champion Florida Gators and their outspoken coach, Steve Spurrier.

Alabama was coached by Gene Stallings, who was about as close a disciple of Bryant as the Crimson Tide could have hired. But it had been a long road to get here. Two head coaches, Ray Perkins and Bill Curry, had come and gone in Tuscaloosa before Alabama hired Stallings in 1990. Stallings had played for Bryant at Texas A&M, followed him to Alabama as an assistant coach, then, after returning to the Aggies as head coach, defeated the Tide in the 1968 Cotton Bowl. Now, in his third season as Alabama's head coach, Stallings had the Crimson Tide within one game of playing for the national title against the swaggering Hurricanes and their Heisman Trophy winner Gino Torretta.

Antonio Langham on his way to the winning touchdown in the 1992 SEC Championship Game. (Photo by Ken Blevins/*Corolla*, courtesy of the UA Office of Student Media)

Florida, however, stood in the way. A young, inexperienced team when the season started, the Gators had scrapped to an 8–3 record and were entirely capable of spoiling Alabama's run for a national championship. A year earlier, a far more veteran Gator team had routed the Tide 35–0 before Stallings and Alabama reeled off ten consecutive victories. Now, the Tide was on a 21-game winning streak.

But what if Alabama lost? Already the talk among SEC coaches and critics of the championship game format was that it would add another obstacle to the conference's chances of having a team in the hunt for a national title. Especially when other conferences had no such "play-in" game before bowl pairings. The theory that SEC teams would "beat each other up" with a division format and a championship game had become a serious topic of discussion.

Kramer well understood the criticism and was reminded of it once the inaugural championship game began and Florida scored first. But Alabama answered with two touchdowns, one on a 3-yard run by Derrick Lassic and another on a 30-yard pass from Jay Barker to Curtis Brown. The Crimson Tide extended the lead to 21–7 with another Lassic touchdown run in the third quarter. But then the Gators mounted a furious comeback, scoring twice to tie the game almost midway through the fourth quarter. Alabama's undefeated season was in jeopardy.

"You had a chance to have a team play for the national championship. Now, all of a sudden if they lose this game, they're gonna lose their shot at a national championship," Kramer told ESPN Films in a documentary called *The Play That Changed College Football*. "I was concerned we had shot ourselves in the foot."

After forcing an Alabama punt, the Gators had the momentum and a first down at their own 21-yard line when quarterback Shane Matthews dropped back to throw. There were just over three minutes left in the game. Thinking he had a receiver open out in the flat, Matthews threw the ball, and suddenly Alabama's Antonio Langham stepped in front of it for an interception and raced 28 yards for a touchdown.

"I still have nightmares thinking about it," Matthews told ESPN.

Langham's TD was the difference in a 28–21 victory and sent Alabama on its way to the Sugar Bowl with a 22-game winning streak and a shot at the program's first national championship since 1979. The victory in the SEC title game did not go unnoticed by other conferences. The game had drawn widespread interest nationally, and it wouldn't be that long before other major conferences added their own postseason championship contests.

29

Domination in New Orleans

It is nearly impossible to adequately describe the remarkable, earth-shattering events that took place in the Louisiana Superdome in New Orleans on the evening of January 1, 1993. It was not *just* a football game. It was not simply a battle to decide it all between the nation's top-two-ranked, undefeated college football teams, both riding long winning streaks. That would, of course, have been enough to give this game a significant place in history. But it was so much more than that.

This was a comeuppance so profound, a humiliation so nationally cheered, a victory so satisfying that in the long, storied history of Alabama football, there has never been anything quite like it. An argument could be made that The Crimson Tide's stunning 1926 Rose Bowl victory over heavily favored Washington might rank near it, or perhaps the Tide's curb-stomping of Tim Tebow's defending national champion Florida Gators in the 2009 Southeastern Conference championship game, or any number of other landmark victories that are now firmly etched into Crimson Tide legend.

But this . . . this was something else. And to understand it, it is necessary to consider the unmitigated swagger of the Miami Hurricanes, the team Alabama was facing on this New Year's Day night in front of nearly 77,000 people in the Superdome and a massive national television audience of millions. Alabama, to be sure, was not your usual underdog. In the weeks since the Crimson Tide's 28–21 SEC championship game victory over Florida—when Antonio Langham jumped in front of a Shane Matthews pass and raced back 28 yards for a game-winning touchdown—Bama coach Gene Stallings had refused to publicly accept the underdog role. His team was 12–0, had the nation's top-ranked defense, one of the best rushing attacks in the nation, had come through a tough SEC schedule unscathed, and was working on a 22-game winning streak.

But almost no one outside his own team and die-hard Alabama fans was listening, and it had everything to do with the Hurricanes, who not only had an outlaw reputation for intimidating and bullying opponents, they had the results to back it up. The Hurricanes had owned the 1980s, winning national championships in 1983, 1987, and 1989 (including a 33–25 win over Alabama in the Sugar Bowl), and they had begun the '90s in much the same fashion—going 12–0 in 1991 for their fourth national title. Now, as defending champions, Miami, led by Heisman Trophy-winner Gino Torretta at quarterback, was on a 29-game winning streak. Judging by their trash talk, which was business as usual for the Hurricanes, Alabama was simply another overrated team that would be dispatched quickly in the Superdome. Or so it seemed, judging by the behavior of Miami players leading up to the game.

During one press conference in New Orleans, Hurricanes wideout Lamar Thomas, considered one of the fastest receivers in the nation, placed his two national championship rings (from 1989 and 1991) on the table beside the microphone and proceeded to declare that the third one to come would be "icing on the cake." (As *Sports Illustrated*'s Austin Murphy wrote after the game: "Instead he wound up with egg on his face.")

For now, though, Thomas kept up the rhetoric, saying he was part of "the best receiving corps probably ever assembled," and taking a shot at the Alabama defense's penchant for zone coverage. "Real men play man," he said. "Anytime we get a team in man-to-man, it's unfair."

Even when the Hurricanes were claiming not to trash-talk, they were, actually, trash-talking.

"I'll do my talking on the field. It's part of our game to dominate and intimidate," Miami linebacker Micheal Barrow told reporters. And then he refused to give the Crimson Tide any credit. "Nobody has my respect. It has to be earned. We've seen on film plenty of times how our opponents have destroyed other teams. But in order to be the best, you've got to play the best, and that's Miami."

As Barrow, Thomas, and the entire Hurricane team would find out soon enough—America would, indeed, see the best team in the nation in the Superdome that night. And it wasn't from Miami.

"In all my years, I've never heard such stuff," Alabama defensive coordinator Bill Oliver said after the game. "They laughed at us when we were warming up. Imagine that."

Once the game began, the laughter stopped. The Hurricanes ran smack up against a Bama team that couldn't care less about Lamar Thomas's championship rings, or Micheal Barrow's empty rhetoric, or Gino Torretta's Heisman Trophy, or Miami's winning streak. With All-Americans Eric Curry and John Copeland bookending either side of the defensive line, and joined by James Gregory, Lemanski Hall, Derrick Oden, Antonio London, Antonio Langham, George Teague, Willie Gaston, Chris Donnelly, and Sam Shade, among others, the Crimson Tide's defense swarmed all over Miami.

Torretta, who had thrown for more than 3,000 yards two years in a row, could do

Alabama's Chris Donnelly puts the brakes on Miami quarterback Gino Torretta. (Photo by Ken Blevins/*Corolla*, courtesy of the UA Office of Student Media)

nothing about the onslaught. When he wasn't running for his life, he was throwing to receivers who could not get open in the Tide's lockdown coverage. And late in the first quarter, it got even worse. Torretta saw something he had never seen. Alabama brought all eleven defensive players to the line of scrimmage. This was no disguise in coverage, as the Crimson Tide had worked to perfection throughout the year. The was a straight-up challenge to a quarterback who was good at reading defenses but found nothing he could recognize here. Confused, he called an audible and overthrew a receiver down the sideline. On the next play, with the Tide defenders again all up on the line, he called a time-out.

Miami players had talked a good game. Alabama was playing one.

The Crimson Tide took a 13–6 lead at halftime, and then came out in the third quarter and just took the game away from Miami. On the Hurricanes' first play from scrimmage in the third quarter, Alabama defensive back Tommy Johnson intercepted a Torretta pass and took it down to Miami's 20-yard line. Six plays later, the Tide's Derrick Lassic ran it into the end zone from the 1-yard line. The extra point made it Alabama 20, Miami 6. On the next Miami series, Bama once again brought all eleven defenders up front. Torretta threw across the middle, and the Tide's George Teague intercepted it, rolled to his right, then high-stepped it down the sidelines to the end zone. The pick-six touchdown and an extra point increased the lead to 27–6, and the rout was on.

But an even more sensational play came on Miami's next series, with the Hurricanes at their own 11-yard line. Torretta dropped back and threw a perfect strike down the sideline to Lamar Thomas. Already behind Alabama's defense, Thomas sped toward the goal line, but Teague, several yards behind him, caught the Miami receiver from behind, stripped the ball away from him near the goal line, and turned back up field with it. An Alabama offside penalty negated the play, but Teague's rundown of Thomas had prevented what would have been an 89-yard Miami touchdown. The Hurricanes were forced to take the penalty (declining it would have given Alabama the ball), and the ball was placed on Miami's 16-yard line. No touchdown, and in its place, only silence from Lamar Alexander, the big-talking receiver who had come into the game, like his teammates, with a lot of swagger and now, as television cameras showed, retreated to the bench and draped a towel over his head.

"The agony of Lamar Thomas," ABC play-by-play announcer Keith Jackson told the viewing audience. "He knows full well how big that previous play was."

Early in the fourth quarter, Miami's All-American kick returner and receiver Kevin Williams scored on a 78-yard punt return, but this game was all but over. Alabama's Derrick Lassic scored on a 6-yard touchdown run later in the quarter, and Alabama won it 34–13. Lassic, who carried the ball 28 times for 135 yards and two touchdowns, was named the game's most valuable player. Alabama quarterback Jay Barker had just thrown for 18 yards the entire game, but no one cared. The Tide's running game churned up 267 yards, more than enough to keep Miami's offense off the field—that is, when Bama's defense wasn't out there giving Torretta and his team fits.

Although Torretta threw for 278 yards, much of it was after Alabama controlled the game. And his three interceptions were costly. The fact that Miami could not establish a rushing game against the Tide's defensive line (with 18 carries for just 48 yards) also doomed the Hurricanes.

Alabama had won its first national championship since 1979, and perhaps just as important, its first since Paul "Bear" Bryant roamed the sidelines. But Tide fans were far from the only ones cheering.

"The only thing better than watching Miami lose is watching it lose bad," wrote *Sports Illustrated* columnist Rick Reilly. "The high-decibel Hurricanes turned out to be mere blowhards."

PART FIVE

A MODERN DYNASTY—NICK SABAN'S CRIMSON TIDE

30

The Arrival

Nick Saban didn't just quietly slip into town to take over the Alabama football program on January 3, 2007. Far from it. Several hundred people cheered wildly as a University of Alabama jet with Saban and his wife, Terry, touched down at Tuscaloosa Regional Airport. When the Sabans walked through the crowd, shaking hands and acknowledging the joyous reception, one woman who had a bit too much to drink kissed the coach on the cheek, then hugged him tightly around the neck before a state trooper pulled her away. Later that day, according to news reports, she was arrested for driving under the influence.

Aside from getting drunk (and most didn't), Alabama fans could be forgiven for perhaps an over-the-top celebration of Saban's arrival. This was a proud program in need of a turnaround. And Tide fans, who know their football, knew they were getting an outstanding football coach who had done wonders in rebuilding LSU's program—leading the Tigers to a national championship—before leaving for a two-year stint with the Miami Dolphins.

Still, Saban faced a major challenge in Tuscaloosa. It had been 14 years since Gene Stallings and the Crimson Tide had won the national championship in a January 1, 1993, beatdown of Miami in the Sugar Bowl. Since then, the program had gone through NCAA sanctions, and a carousel of coaches, having never made it back to the elite stature it once enjoyed. There had been some glorious moments in the meantime, including a 1999 SEC championship season led by one of the program's greatest running backs, Shaun Alexander. But they were too few and far between. The last coach, former Alabama quarterback Mike Shula, was respected by Tide fans, but, with the exception of a 10–2 season in 2005, his teams were never able to break out of the pack in the SEC. Shula's overall record during four years as coach was 26–23. (He was fired at the end of the 2006 regular season and did not coach the Tide in an Independence Bowl game against Oklahoma State that year.)

Alabama head coach Nick Saban. (Photo courtesy of *The Crimson White* and the UA Office of Student Media)

Now, with Saban, expectations were sky-high. That fall, in Saban's first season at Alabama, the Crimson Tide went 7–6, an inauspicious start, but it included a 30–24 Independence Bowl victory over Colorado and set the stage for much bigger things to come. The new era began in earnest with the signing of the 2008 recruiting class, one of the greatest ever in college football. It included Julio Jones, Mark Ingram, Mark Barron,

Dont'a Hightower, Marcell Dareus, Courtney Upshaw, Damion Square, Barrett Jones, Terrence Cody, Robert Lester, Michael Williams, and Brad Smelley, among others. Five would become first-round NFL draft choices, 12 would make NFL rosters, one (Ingram) would win a Heisman Trophy, and several remain today among the top players in pro football.

Above: Alabama's Terrence Cody blocks Tennessee's field goal attempt on the last play of the game to preserve Alabama's undefeated season in 2009. (Photo by John Michael Simpson/*The Crimson White*, courtesy of the UA Office of Student Media)

Left: Julio Jones fights for yardage against Tennessee, 2009. (Photo courtesy of *The Crimson White* and the UA Office of Student Media)

Part Five

"When I got there [at Alabama], we kept hearing that they had won 12 national championships," Damion Square said as he prepared for the NFL draft back in 2013. "But in my mind, I'm thinking that the last one was in 1992. That's a long time. They had so much pride about that title game in 1992. But I'm thinking, 'We've got to get something new around here.'"

Square, a talented, big defensive end at 6-foot-3, 285 pounds, and his teammates set about doing just that—bringing new hardware to a dusty trophy case. They would be part of a class that won 61 games over five seasons (2008–2012), tying a record set by Nebraska in the 1990s, and standing alone with three BCS national championships and two SEC titles in that span.

31

A Heisman at Last

By 2009, Alabama had won just about everything there was to win in major college football. There had been glorious bowl victories stretching from Los Angeles to Miami. There were trophy cases full of national and conference championships. There were two Outland trophies, a Lott Trophy, a Lombardi Award, a Jim Thorpe Award, a Johnny Unitas Golden Arm, a Butkus Award (and another coming soon), a couple of dozen Hall of Fame honors, and enough All-American and All-Conference honors to start an army.

But something major was missing. Not once had an Alabama player won a Heisman Trophy. It seemed inconceivable. The first Heisman had been handed out in 1935, and since that time, players like Harry Gilmer, Bart Starr, Joe Namath, Leroy Jordan, Ken Stabler, Ozzie Newsome, Johnny Musso, Cornelius Bennett, Derrick Thomas, Bobby Humphrey, David Palmer, and Shaun Alexander—to just name a few—had played at Alabama. Yet, not one of them had won the famous stiff-armed trophy signifying college football's best player.

Mark Ingram, a fast, durable, power running back from Flint, Michigan, was among the top recruits Nick Saban signed in 2008, in what has been called one of the greatest recruiting classes in college football history. As a backup to starter Glen Coffee in his freshman year, Ingram gained nearly 750 yards rushing and was named to the SEC's 2008 All-Freshmen team. It was Nick Saban's second year as head coach at Alabama, with the Tide rolling undefeated through the 2008 regular season before losing back-to-back postseason games—a 31–20 loss to Florida in the SEC title game and an unexpected 31–17 loss to Utah in the Sugar Bowl.

But Ingram, son of former New York Giants receiver Mark Ingram Sr., and Alabama were just getting started. In the 2009 opener, Ingram gained 150 yards rushing and scored two fourth-quarter touchdowns in a 34–24 victory over Virginia Tech in Atlanta's Georgia

Mark Ingram scores against Auburn, 2008. (Photo by Drew Hoover/*The Crimson White*, courtesy of the UA Office of Student Media)

Dome—winning the Chick-Fil-A Kickoff Classic's player of the game award and setting the tone for the season.

Other big games would follow: Ingram rushed for 140 yards against Kentucky, 172 against Ole Miss, 144 against LSU, 149 against Mississippi State, and a whopping 246 yards on 24 carries against South Carolina. Although Auburn held him to just 30 yards rushing, the Crimson Tide came from behind to defeat the Tigers 26–21 on a 79-yard, 15-play drive in the fourth quarter, to preserve an undefeated season.

As the season had worn on, Ingram steadily moved up in Heisman conversation, but there was plenty of talk after the Iron Bowl that maybe he had lost his chance. The good news for Alabama and Ingram was that the deadline for Heisman voting would come after the SEC title game.

In a rematch with the undefeated Gators, Alabama won in a rout 32–13, in what amounted to a play-in victory to face Texas in the Bowl Championship Series National Championship Game, set for January 7, 2010, at Rose Bowl Stadium in Pasadena, California. But first, there was the matter of the Heisman to consider.

Ingram had an outstanding game against Florida, rushing for 113 yards and three touchdowns, and another 75 yards receiving. For the season, the sophomore from Flint would finish with 1,658 yards and 17 rushing touchdowns, along with another 334 receiving yards, including three TDs. Perhaps most notable of all, more than 1,000 of his 1,992 all-purpose yards had come after contact.

On the evening of December 12, in a nationally televised ESPN broadcast from New York, Ingram was announced as the 2009 Heisman Trophy winner. It had been the closest vote in the 75-year history of the award, with Stanford running back Toby Gerhart second in the balloting.

"I'm a little overwhelmed right now," Ingram said as he accepted the award, his voice breaking as he saw his mother in tears in the audience. "I'm just so excited to bring Alabama their first Heisman winner. . . . Everybody in the Alabama family has had my back, supporting me."

For Ingram, who would be back for one more season before beginning an outstanding career with the NFL's New Orleans Saints, there was still unfinished business as 2009 came to an end. He and Alabama would be flying out West soon to take on the unbeaten Texas Longhorns. The setting was a place where Alabama's storied tradition had truly begun: Rose Bowl Stadium.

32

Perfection. a 14–0 Season, and a Dynasty Is Born

In the 2008 SEC championship game in Atlanta, Alabama had taken a lead into the fourth quarter and let it slip away against quarterback Tim Tebow and the eventual national champion Florida Gators. It was one of those "what could have been" moments that gnawed at the Crimson Tide players and coaches all year. So when a rematch came around on December 5, 2009, Alabama was as ready as it had ever been for a football game.

"Do your job and do it every play in the game," Nick Saban told his team in a moment captured in a UA Athletics video just as players were ready to leave the locker room. "So let's go dominate these guys for 60 minutes." And that is exactly what they did.

Tebow and his No. 1-ranked, unbeaten Gators, as it turned out, had no chance against No. 2 Alabama, which also came into the game unbeaten. The Crimson Tide destroyed Florida 32–13 in a game that left no doubt who the real No. 1 team was in America. Quarterback Greg McElroy had the finest game of his career, throwing for 239 yards and a touchdown against the unbeaten Gators, while Mark Ingram rushed for 113 yards and three touchdowns. McElroy would be named the game's most valuable player, and Ingram would make history a week later by becoming the first Alabama player to ever win a Heisman Trophy. Across the field, Tebow, who had won the Heisman as a sophomore two years earlier, was in tears as the clock wound down in the fourth quarter.

For Alabama, with a 13–0 record, it was on to the BCS National Championship Game against Texas. Making it even more special was the fact that the game, scheduled for January 7, 2010, would be played in Rose Bowl Stadium, where Johnny Mack Brown, Pooley Hubert, Dixie Howell, Don Hutson, Harry Gilmer, and so many other Crimson

Tide stars had earned legendary victories in the first half of the twentieth century. Now there was more history to be made, and the Crimson Tide delivered.

The Texas Longhorns came into the national title game with the nation's best rushing defense statistically, but they were no match for Alabama's running game. Alabama backs Mark Ingram and Trent Richardson each rushed for more than 100 yards and combined for four touchdowns. (Ingram ran for 116 rushing yards and two touchdowns, and Trent Richardson added 109 yards and two TDs of his own.) Alabama's defense, led by Courtney Upshaw, Mark Barron, Eryk Anders, Rolando McClain, Javier Arenas, and Marcell Dareus also had a big night. Dareus also added to the scoreboard—intercepting a shovel pass and returning it 28 yards for a touchdown in the second quarter.

After trailing 24–6 at halftime, Texas backup quarterback Garrett Gilbert, filling in for Longhorn starter Colt McCoy, who was injured early in the game, helped the Longhorns back to within three points in the fourth quarter. But two turnovers led to Bama touchdowns, and the Crimson Tide took a 37–21 victory, won the national championship—its first since 1979—and left California with a 14–0 record, the most wins in a single season in school history.

"I wanted everybody to know, this is not the end. This is the beginning," Saban said during a national championship celebration back in Tuscaloosa nine days after the game. Truer words, as they say, have never been spoken.

33

Devastation in Tuscaloosa and an Inspiring Journey to the 2011 National Championship

The Alabama Crimson Tide had a lot more to play for than just championships or trophies in 2011. When an EF-4 tornado roared through Tuscaloosa shortly after 5 p.m. on April 27, it brought death and destruction on an unimaginable scale—devastating a city and galvanizing a recovery effort. The massive wedge tornado cut a path up to a mile wide and seven miles long through Tuscaloosa, killing 53 people, injuring at least 1,000 others, and destroying or damaging more than 5,000 homes. Among the dead were six University of Alabama students. All told, 253 people died in Alabama that day from a record 62 tornadoes that touched down in the state.

Suddenly, football seem unimportant. What was needed was an all-out commitment by the community to pull together, help those in need, and rebuild. Volunteers by the thousands responded, including Nick Saban and his football team. The coach and his players pitched in with recovery efforts across the city in the immediate aftermath, and the program committed to helping rebuild houses for some of those who had lost them. Among the UA students killed in the storm was Ashley Harrison, who was taking shelter with her boyfriend, Tide long snapper Carson Tinker, in the closet of an off-campus house when it took a direct hit from the tornado.

Tinker survived being thrown 50 feet from where the house once stood, but he, his university, his team, and most especially the families of the victims would never be the same. The silver lining in such a horrific tragedy was that it brought the entire city together.

Nick's Kids, a charitable foundation run by Saban and his wife, Terry, made a significant impact, as well, donating more than $1 million to help rebuild the city.

At a memorial service on campus, Saban said the natural disaster, and the response by the community, "should be a lesson to us all. That we should help others. We should not need a tragedy to inspire us to try to help others. We should serve other people all the time."

He also announced the team would wear ribbons on their helmets throughout the 2011 season in memory of the victims and in recognition of the thousands who had helped in the aftermath. It was clear that while football paled in comparison to the life-and-death events of that tragic day in April, it could nevertheless help lift spirits in Tuscaloosa.

Once the season got underway, it became increasingly obvious that Alabama and LSU were separating themselves not only from the rest of the SEC West, but also from other teams nationally, as well. The Tigers, ranked No. 1, and the Crimson Tide, at No. 2, were thundering through their schedules, routing good teams and moving ever closer to a monumental showdown.

Something had to give as both teams, with identical 8–0 records, prepared to meet in what was being billed as "The Game of the Century," a lofty moniker for a regular-season contest. But it wasn't all hype. Alabama had overwhelmed its opponents by a combined 315–55 points. Only Penn State, in what would become Joe Paterno's last year as coach,

Trent Richardson scores against Penn State.
(Photo by John Michael Simpson/*The Crimson White*, courtesy of the UA Office of Student Media)

had come within 16 points of the Crimson Tide, losing 27-11 at home to Alabama in the second game of the season. LSU had a similar monstrous run, outscoring the opposition 314–92.

The buildup to the game in Tuscaloosa—with both teams having two weeks to prepare—took on a championship-like atmosphere. ESPN, which wasn't even broadcasting the contest, treated it like a Super Bowl, with two weeks' worth of reports from each campus, and then sending its College Football Gameday crew to Tuscaloosa for the final three days.

Ultimately, it would give CBS, the network broadcasting the game, its highest-rated regular-season college football telecast in 22 years, dating back to a Miami–Notre Dame game in 1989. In the end, for Alabama and LSU—two teams used to scoring at will against other opponents—it would be one of the most intense defensive battles in college football history. Not even 60 minutes of football were enough. The game stretched into overtime with LSU defeating Alabama by a field goal. The scoreboard read 9–6, two numbers that might usually indicate a boring game, but not this one. It seemed every play counted, and from the press box, at least, the tension seemed almost unbearable as the game progressed.

For Alabama, it was a game of missed opportunities, literally. The Crimson Tide made only two of six field goals, while outgaining LSU in yardage.

"It's going to eat me up a little bit, but it's not like we played a sorry team," Alabama running back Trent Richardson said after the game. "They're ranked No. 1 for a reason. They're a good ball team. We both went out there and battled. So, it's not the end."

Richardson and Alabama would, indeed, get a second chance at LSU, after the Tide finished the season with consecutive victories over Mississippi State, Georgia Southern, and Auburn. Despite the LSU loss, Alabama had only dropped from second to third in the BCS rankings. (The rankings were based on a combination of two separate polls and six different computer rankings.) And soon afterward, Alabama moved back into the No. 2 spot, with both Stanford and Oklahoma State, two strong contenders, suffering losses.

LSU went on to defeat SEC East winner Georgia in the conference championship game, but unfortunately for the Tigers, Alabama would be waiting for them at the BCS National Championship Game in New Orleans. Although there was controversy nationally over the fact that two SEC teams would meet in a rematch for the national championship, Alabama's players and coaches were not backing down. The best two teams in the nation just so happened to be in the SEC. And that was that.

"We are not going to apologize for being in the game," Saban said. "Our players created this opportunity and they deserve it. That's the system, and according to the system, we should be there."

Sweet Revenge

LSU had won nine consecutive football games at the Mercedes-Benz Superdome, including national championships in 2003 and 2007. But there would be no LSU celebration this time: Alabama's defense dominated the Tigers, not even allowing them to cross midfield until the fourth quarter. Meanwhile, Bama was moving the ball on offense, though not getting it into the end zone. Placekicker Jeremy Shelley tied an all-time bowl record with five field goals to put the Tide up 15–0 after three quarters. Then it finally happened: Bama's Trent Richardson bounced off tackle and broke free on a 34-yard run down the sideline with 4:36 left in the game—scoring the only touchdown by either team in eight quarters and an overtime of football, spanning two games. The 21–0 victory (and it never seemed even that close) earned Alabama its second national championship in three years.

Alabama wide receiver Kevin Norwood leaps for a catch in the 2012 BCS National Championship Game. (Photo by John Michael Simpson/ *The Crimson White*, courtesy of the UA Office of Student Media)

Tide quarterback AJ McCarron was named the game's most valuable offensive player, throwing for 234 yards, while linebacker Courtney Upshaw took most valuable defensive player honors. Richardson, who had finished third in the Heisman Trophy race, rushed for 96 yards on 20 carries, and the game's only touchdown. "I'm really proud of the way our team competed in this game today," Saban said. "To have two teams as good as our two teams in the same division, in the same conference, is pretty unique. They were the only team that beat us. I'm really proud of what our players did in coming back (after the regular-season loss) and winning this game."

34

An SEC Thriller

Twenty years after Alabama won the Southeastern Conference's first-ever postseason championship game in 1992 and went on to win the national title afterward, the stakes were just as high as the Crimson Tide and Georgia prepared to battle in the 2012 version of the conference title contest.

With Alabama ranked No. 2—and fresh from a 49–0 dismantling of Auburn, in which the Tide had emptied its bench to keep it from being an even worse rout—and Georgia at No. 3, the winner was assured of moving on to face undefeated and top-ranked Notre Dame in the BCS National Championship Game on January 7, 2013, in Miami Gardens, Florida. But that could wait.

No game, not even one for the national championship, could overshadow the SEC thriller that the Crimson Tide and Bulldogs played on a magical night in Atlanta's Georgia Dome. When it was finally done, Alabama had defeated Georgia 32–28 in a come-from-behind battle that was not decided until the clock ran out on the Bulldogs at the Alabama 5-yard line. Georgia quarterback Aaron Murray, operating with no time-outs after an 80-yard drive, threw a pass intended for receiver Malcolm Mitchell in the end zone. The ball was tipped, instead, by Alabama linebacker C. J. Mosley and caught by Georgia flanker Chris Conley, who fell to the ground inbounds, as the clock ticked to zero.

Alabama had captured its twenty-third SEC championship in a nail-biter of a finish. "This conference will test your mettle," Alabama coach Nick Saban said after the game. "We beat a really good team out there today."

And so they did.

"It was a little scary," Alabama nose guard Jesse Williams said, referring to Georgia's final drive. "I thought the clock was moving twice as slow as usual." With the final seconds gone, the celebration was on for the Crimson Tide, which overcame a 21–10 third-quarter deficit and improved its record to 12–1. The team would now get to play for a third national championship in four years.

"We don't talk about legacies and dynasties," said Alabama center Barrett Jones. "We talk about this season. About now." Jones, who sustained a foot injury early in the game, never missed a play but nevertheless had to use crutches to walk through the locker room afterward. His battle through adversity summed up the attitude of his entire team.

Alabama had won this one in the trenches, amassing an SEC championship game record of 350 yards rushing, along with key passes that included a 55-yard AJ McCarron-to-Amari Cooper touchdown strike with just 3:15 left in the contest.

"This game is going to last a long time as one of the great SEC championships," said Cooper, a standout freshman who finished with seven receptions for 127 yards. "I'm glad I could be part of it."

Following a couple of McCarron turnovers in the first half, including an interception and a fumble, Alabama turned to the rushing game to establish control over the Bulldogs' defensive line. Eddie Lacy was named the game's most valuable player after a dominating performance that included 181 yards on just 20 carries (a 9.1-yards-per-carry average) and two touchdowns.

Bama's T. J. Yeldon also had a big game with 153 yards on 25 carries, and a touchdown, giving him exactly 1,000 yards for the season. Yeldon and Lacy's rushing totals, combined with McCarron's 162 yards through the air, gave Alabama 512 total yards, a remarkable showing, considering the future NFL talent—like Jarvis Jones, Alec Ogletree, and Bacarri Rambo—on Georgia's defense. For the Bulldogs, Murray went 18–33 for 265 yards, one touchdown, and one interception. Overall, his team totaled 394 yards, including 113 rushing.

"You know, it was a knock-down, drag-out fight and everybody swung to the end," UGA coach Mark Richt said afterward. "We had a chance at the end. We just didn't get it done."

The Bulldogs had played outstanding football and simply came up short against an Alabama team that now turned its sights on an old nemesis: The Notre Dame Fighting Irish.

35

Rout of the Irish

Notre Dame had the No. 1 ranking, an undefeated record, and the majority of their fans inside South Florida's Sun Life Stadium on a January night were confident that the Fighting Irish were about to "wake up the echoes" of their storied program.

It didn't take long for that dream to turn into a nightmare, beginning with a decision, after winning the coin toss, to defer on offense until the second half. It was the first mistake of many for Notre Dame, although ultimately it wouldn't matter.

It was clear from Alabama's opening 82-yard drive—the longest one Notre Dame's highly-touted defense had given up all season—that the Irish had no chance in this game. It only got worse from there.

The Crimson Tide routed Notre Dame 42–14 before a crowd of 80,120, many paying more than $1,000 per ticket, on January 7, 2013. Nearly thirty million television viewers saw the same thing: this was domination on a grand stage. The result was Alabama's second consecutive Bowl Championship Series national title and the Tide's third in the past four years.

"People talk about how the most difficult thing is to win your first championship," Alabama coach Nick Saban said after the game. "Really, the most difficult is to win the next one because there's always a feeling of entitlement."

It was obvious that Saban, his assistant coaches, and his players had spent a month since the team's SEC championship game victory over Georgia preparing as if they'd won nothing yet. Although the Tide came into the BCS title game as a solid favorite, despite weeks of hype from analysts predicting this would be close, the team played as if it had something to prove. And it easily accomplished that goal, making a strong case that the rest of the nation had yet to catch up to the talent, speed, and physical play of an elite SEC team.

Part Five

Alabama led this one 28–0 at halftime, a show of dominance so profound that when asked by an ESPN reporter at halftime what adjustments his team needed to make, Notre Dame coach Brian Kelly candidly joked: "Maybe Alabama doesn't come back in the second half. It's all Alabama. I mean, we can't tackle them right now. Who knows why. They're big and physical."

Eddie Lacy scores against Notre Dame in the 2013 BCS National Championship Game. (From *The Crimson White*, courtesy of the UA Office of Student Media)

After the game, Kelly acknowledged that, despite the fact the Irish came into the game with the No. 1 ranking and a 12–0 record, they were not yet at Alabama's level.

"We've got to get physically stronger, continue to close the gap there, and just overall you need to see what it looks like," Kelly said. "Our guys clearly know what it looks like. When I say 'know what it looks like,' a championship football team. They're (Alabama) back-to-back national champs. So that's what it looks like."

But it had not always been that way between these two teams. Notre Dame had once had the upper hand. Way back in the 1973 Sugar Bowl, Notre Dame had defeated Paul "Bear" Bryant and the Crimson Tide 24–23 in a highly anticipated first-ever meeting between the two teams, and the Irish since that time had built a 5–1 record against the Tide. And there were still plenty of Bama fans around who blamed Notre Dame for the fact that an undefeated Crimson Tide team in 1966 had not been awarded the national championship. Voters in both the *Associated Press* and *United Press International* polls had selected the Irish as national champs that year, even though Notre Dame had played to a 10–10 tie late in the season against Michigan State and had not accepted a bowl bid.

It had, of course, been decades since that 1966 season, but old memories—including bad ones—die hard.

But only the Irish would have bad memories from this 2013 BCS national champion-ship game. For Alabama, it was a night of stars: Quarterback AJ McCarron completed 20 of 28 passes for 264 yards and four touchdowns, while Tide running backs Eddie Lacy and T. J. Yeldon ran over the Irish for more than 100 yards each (140 yards for Lacy and 108 for Yeldon). Lacy, who rushed for one touchdown and caught a short pass and powered into the end zone with two jaw-dropping spin moves for the other, was named the game's most valuable offensive player.

Overall, Alabama totaled 529 yards to 302 for Notre Dame (much of that coming after the outcome was decided in the second half). "We came out, started fast, and finished strong like we always preach," McCarron said.

Freshman wide receiver Amari Cooper, playing in his hometown, also had a big night, hauling in six receptions for 105 yards and two touchdowns.

"This is what I came to Alabama for," said Cooper, who two years later would become the No. 4 overall pick in the 2015 NFL draft, then become the first rookie in Oakland Raiders history to break the 1,000-yard receiving mark.

Notre Dame had entered the game with the No. 1 scoring defense in the country. By the time the battle was won, Alabama's defense had taken over the No. 1 scoring defense ranking in addition to the national title.

Tide linebacker C. J. Mosley was named the defensive player of the game for a stellar performance that contributed to holding Notre Dame to just 32 yards rushing.

But it was Alabama's offensive line that drew the most accolades. Led by All-American center Barrett Jones, who played with torn ligaments in his left foot, the Tide overpowered Notre Dame's vaunted defensive front line and turned the Irish's award-winning line-backer Manti Te'o into a nonfactor.

"It started in the locker room," Tide offensive tackle D. J. Fluker said. "We had the mindset that we were going to come out here and dominate. We were all fired up today."

It began with the Crimson Tide's first set of downs. Alabama took less than three minutes to drive 82 yards, highlighted by runs from Lacy and a 29-yard pass from McCarron to Kevin Norwood. Lacy took it the final 20 yards into the end zone. A Jeremy Shelley extra point made it 7–0.

Notre Dame had given up just two rushing touchdowns in the red zone all season. Alabama's scoring drive made a statement that the Irish were facing an entirely different opponent on this night. The drive was the first sign of trouble for Notre Dame fans, who comprised an estimated 60 to 65 percent of the game's attendance.

"They had more fans here," McCarron said. "They were loud during warm-ups. We knew we had to get the crowd out of it so we could hear each other, communicate and talk and make the game easier for us."

On their next possession, McCarron and the offense moved 61 yards in 10 plays, alternating between rushes from Lacy and short passes to Amari Cooper and Marvin Shinn. A 3-yard touchdown pass from McCarron to tight end Michael Williams completed the drive. Shelley's extra point made it Alabama 14, Notre Dame 0.

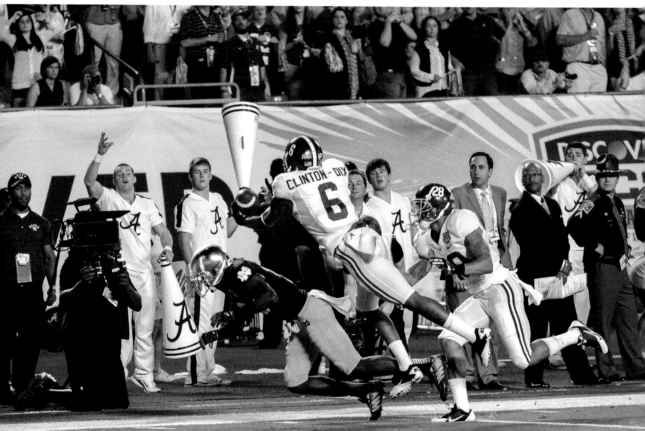

The Crimson Tide's Ha Ha Clinton-Dix dives for a spectacular interception against Notre Dame. (Photo by Austin Bigoney/*The Crimson White*, courtesy of the UA Office of Student Media)

Minutes later, with the first quarter winding down, the Tide was back on the Irish goal line after long passes from McCarron to Kevin Norwood and Amari Cooper. T. J. Yeldon's 1-yard plunge into the end zone just as the second quarter began capped an 80-yard drive and, with an extra-point kick from Shelley, gave Alabama a commanding 21–0 lead.

But it was another Crimson Tide touchdown just before halftime that seemed to seal the outcome. After runs by Yeldon and a 27-yard strike from McCarron to Cooper, Alabama had a first down on Notre Dame's 11-yard line with under a minute left in the half. McCarron dropped back, threw a short pass over the middle to Lacy, and the standout running back used two spin moves to get past Irish defenders and into the end zone. A Shelley extra point made it 28–0.

"I feel like the game changed at halftime, or right before halftime," McCarron said. "The touchdown pass to Eddie, when he bounced off two guys and put it in. I think that kind of took the life out of them."

It was all but over. Alabama would go on to win the game 42–14 and secure its third national championship in four seasons. There were more to come.

Part Five

36

Derrick Henry's Journey to the Heisman Trophy

It was that moment in a blowout football game when the clock isn't running fast enough to catch up with fans walking toward the exits. When boredom has replaced drama. When the last hot dogs have been sold, and families lucky enough to get seats together are talking more about traffic leaving the stadium than about any action inside it.

On the field, however, the coaches, players, and officials are not done. Even if they would like to be. Not on this night.

It was October 19, 2013, and this was a yawner of a football game as the clock fell below two minutes at Alabama's Bryant-Denny Stadium. The Crimson Tide led Arkansas 45–0, and there was little left to do but run the ball and watch the seconds disappear. Already, Nick Saban and his assistant coaches had emptied the bench, playing everyone with a helmet and shoulder pads.

One of the backups, Derrick Henry, the big, fast freshman running back who had been a national high school sensation, had received fewer than a handful of carries as the game wound down. Four other Alabama backs—T. J. Yeldon, Kenyan Drake, Jalston Fowler, and Dee Hart—had entered the game before Henry.

Now, in mop-up duty, Henry took a handoff from backup quarterback Blake Sims on first down and rushed five yards into the pile of bodies in front of him, stretching the ball to the Crimson Tide's 20-yard line. The clock continued to run. No one, least of all Arkansas, which wanted no more of this torture, had any notion of stopping the clock.

So Bama lined up again on second down, and everyone in the stadium knew it would be another handoff. Saban would never allow the Tide to throw a pass with this kind of lead so late in the game. Critics have said a lot of not-so-nice things about him, but running up the score is not one of them. Saban always respected the opponent, and the Tide was probably one more play away from taking a knee, then heading for the locker room.

Only, it didn't turn out that way.

Henry took the second-down handoff with 1:15 left in the game, cut back toward the left corner, and raced down the sidelines, with Arkansas defenders helplessly in pursuit behind him.

"Two hundred thirty-eight pounds and 80 yards. Touchdown! Whoa!" ESPN play-by-play announcer Brad Nessler told his audience, adding moments later, "Holy smokes. A two-play drive, 80 of which is the freshman from Yulee, Florida, and he looked like he was heading to Florida down the sideline. Man, oh man."

It was the first touchdown of Henry's career at Alabama, and it was a spectacular one, ending the scoring (with an extra point added) at 52–0. "It shouldn't be possible for someone that large to run that fast," said Marc Torrence, who was standing on the sideline, covering the game for *The Crimson White*, the student newspaper, when Henry swept by on his way to the end zone.

There would be many more jaw-dropping runs to follow for the 6-foot-3, 238-pound running back. Before he was done at Alabama, Henry would shatter many of the school's rushing and scoring records, and break a few SEC records along the way, including the conference's single-season rushing record held by the legendary Herschel Walker.

But on the night of the Arkansas game in 2013, no one could be sure just how far he would go. Henry had gained widespread attention as a high school recruit, setting a national high school rushing record of 12,124 yards at Yulee High School, where he was also a sprinter on the track team. His combination of speed, size, and power was rare.

He graduated early, enrolled at The University of Alabama in January 2013, and was doing well in spring practice before fracturing his fibula in a scrimmage, an injury that sidelined him through the summer but clearly was in the rear-view mirror by the time Henry lined up against Arkansas later that season. His bigger problem, perhaps, was simply the talented roster of running backs at Alabama, where an apprentice sort of platoon system had been used since Saban's arrival, to great success.

One of the backs ahead of Henry on the depth chart was Kenyan Drake, who didn't let what became a defining moment in Henry's early Alabama career—the touchdown against Arkansas—pass without notice.

"I'm one of Derrick's biggest fans," Drake, now playing for the NFL's Miami Dolphins, said after the game. "That's his favorite thing, to hit the outside corner. I always tell him, 'When you do it, I know you're going to show your speed, so just don't let anyone catch you from behind.' He sure didn't do that."

Nor did he do it any other day. No one was going to catch Henry once he got behind the defense. Long, breakaway runs would become a signature of his Alabama career. The only thing that could stop him, it seemed, was not being on the field. Henry had just 36 carries his freshman season. Two years later there would be *single games* when he had more carries than that. No matter, that first year he made the most of those carries, gaining 382 yards for an impressive 10.6 yards-per-carry average.

Still, for a five-star recruit who had been named *Parade* magazine's Player of the Year and Florida's Mr. Football his senior year in high school, Henry's first season at Alabama had been long and frustrating. ESPN reported that Henry had even quietly contemplated transferring from Alabama but was urged by family and former high school coaches to stick it out, and at least talk to Alabama coaches about it. Whatever the outcome of those conversations in mid-December 2013, it was obvious that things turned around quickly for Henry when Alabama took the field against Oklahoma on January 2, 2014. Henry was given the No. 2 running back position, and he made the most of it, with 161 all-purpose yards and two touchdowns. Those included a 43-yard scoring run in the third quarter and a 61-yard TD in the fourth, when he took a short pass from AJ McCarron, cut through the Sooner defense, and then outran them to the end zone. Alabama lost the game, but Henry had made his mark.

"We decided that he was our second best back going into this game, and we were going to give him an opportunity based on his performance in practice and what he had done, the confidence that he had gained throughout the course of the season in terms of knowing what to do and playing fast," Saban said after the game. "He certainly had an outstanding game tonight, and did a really good job for us, and I think he has a bright future."

As the 2014 season began, Henry, in his sophomore year, was still the No. 2 running back to Yeldon, but by the end of the year it was Henry who led all Crimson Tide rushers with 990 yards and 11 touchdowns, although Yeldon was right behind with 979 yards and an equal 11 TDs. If anything, sharing carries with such a talented running back as Yeldon had helped Henry, not only in his running technique and blocking ability, but also in keeping him fresh for what would be a phenomenal junior season.

Yet, the 2014 season had ended just as 2013, with another crushing loss in the Sugar Bowl. This time it was to Ohio State in the first-ever College Football playoff. Henry, however, had done his part, with 95 yards on 13 carries, a touchdown, and another 54 yards receiving. But Ohio State's running back Ezekiel Elliott had a far bigger game, with 230 yards on 20 carries and two touchdowns, and his team won the game 42–35.

Ohio State would go on to win the national championship in a blowout over Oregon and would be an overwhelming favorite to repeat in 2015. But as college football prognostications often go, the one regarding the Buckeyes' invincibility wouldn't pan out. Ohio State entered the 2015 season as a unanimous No. 1 choice in preseason polls. But Alabama, not the Buckeyes, would be there in the playoffs again in the postseason.

First, however, there was a lot of football to be played, and for the Crimson Tide, Derrick Henry would be at the center of it.

Now, as the featured back with Yeldon off to the NFL, Henry went to work, beginning with 147 yards on just 13 carries and three touchdowns in the Crimson Tide's season opener against Wisconsin. Kenyan Drake, now Henry's backup, had suffered a broken leg early in the 2014 season, and there were lingering questions about how durable he would be in 2015. He answered those doubts with 77 yards rushing, a touchdown, and 48 yards receiving against the Badgers.

Together, Henry and Drake would be a challenging tandem for defenses. But as the season progressed, Henry's workload increased. He was simply running over, around, and through SEC defenses. When he rushed for 210 yards and three touchdowns against LSU on November 7—and the Crimson Tide's defense held the Tigers' Leonard Fournette to just 39 yards on 19 carries—the Heisman Trophy race flipped on its end. Fournette had been a runaway favorite to win the trophy. Now Henry was the favorite, and Fournette's opportunity was done. At least for 2015.

"I'm not really worried about the Heisman," Henry said immediately after the LSU game. "I'm saying that we came out and played. We came out and competed and we beat a great team."

Henry had carried the ball 38 times against LSU. A week later, when Kenyan Drake suffered another injury, this time a broken arm against Mississippi State, Alabama's offense depended more than ever on Henry. He seemed more than up to the challenge. Obsessed with preparation in workouts and practice, Henry only got stronger down the stretch.

He gained 204 yards with two touchdowns against Mississippi State, played sparingly in the next game against Charleston Southern, carried the ball an eye-opening 46 times for 271 yards and a touchdown against Auburn, then added 189 yards and a touchdown on 44 carries against Florida in the SEC title game.

"I can't tell you how proud I am of this guy," Saban said, sitting next to Henry at a news conference after the Florida game. "He's had a phenomenal season, and he deserves every accolade that anyone could ever throw his way."

But was it enough as Heisman voters cast their ballots? Henry broke Herschel Walker's SEC single-season rushing record during the SEC championship game, with 1,986 yards. (Walker rushed for 1,891 yards in 1981.) And Henry's yards had come against eight of the top 50 rushing defenses in the nation. In fact, he had performed his best work against the best—rushing for an average 180 yards per game against the seven ranked opponents Alabama had faced so far. There were other superlatives, as well, including 23 touchdowns, tying the SEC single-season record, and a nation-leading 18 consecutive games with a rushing touchdown.

Late in the day on Monday, December 7, two days after the Florida game, it was announced that Henry, Stanford's all-purpose running back Christian McCaffrey, and Clemson quarterback Deshaun Watson would be heading to New York as Heisman finalists.

Both Henry and Watson would also be heading to the college football playoffs. Clemson, at No. 1, would face No. 4 Oklahoma. And Alabama, ranked second, would face No. 3 Michigan State.

Finally, Henry could take a break from practice and preparation and enjoy the moment.

Winning the Heisman had "always been a dream of mine, so to just be in the conversation with this award is a blessing," Henry told reporters after the announcement. "It's a blessing to have this opportunity to play for this great university, for my teammates and coaches, and to just go out there and play on Saturdays."

Derrick Henry takes off on a 30-yard touchdown run in the rain against Georgia. (Photo by Layton Dudley/*The Crimson White*, courtesy of the UA Office of Student Media)

The first stop for all three Heisman finalists would be at the College Football Hall of Fame in Atlanta, site of the 25th annual Home Depot College Football Awards on Thursday, December 10.

It was Derrick Henry's night.

He picked up all three awards for which he was a finalist, including the Maxwell Award as college football's player of the year, the Walter Camp Player of the Year Award, and the Doak Walker Award as the nation's best running back. Watson won the Davey O'Brien Award as the nation's top quarterback.

It was on to New York, and for Saturday evening, December 12.

Born to teenage parents, Henry had been raised in Yulee, Florida, by his grandmother, Gladys Henry, who had nicknamed him "Shocka" at his birth. After all, Derrick's parents were just 15 and 16 when he was born, and Shocka seemed to be appropriate. It was a nickname that would stick with Derrick Henry throughout his childhood.

Now 81, Gladys Henry was confined to a hospital bed in Jacksonville, Florida, and couldn't make the trip with Henry to New York. But she and a host of family members were watching ESPN's live broadcast of the ceremony, and the room erupted with cheers when Henry was named the 81st winner of the Heisman Trophy.

In attendance at the ceremony were Henry's parents, Stacy Veal and Derrick Henry Sr., Alabama head coach Nick Saban, and running backs coach Burton Burns, among others. Derrick Henry, dapper for this primetime moment in a smart blue suit and crimson-striped tie, gave them all a hug before making his way to the podium for an emotional acceptance speech.

"Mom and Dad, man, my mom, my best friend who brought me into this world, I just want to thank you so much for always being there for me," Henry said, peering past the microphone at his mother, Stacy Veal. "Through my struggles you always heard me. Anytime I was struggling, you were always there for me. I'd call you late at night, you'd be asleep. I know you'd have to be up at 3 o'clock in the morning, but you would answer for me, just to hear what I had to say, and help me get through whatever I would need to get through. To my dad, my No. 1 fan, man, always kept me in sports. Always there for me, day after day, being young and being so supportive, keeping me in sports, I just want to thank you so much, man. Even in the games, every game I played, you was always loud."

Then he turned his thoughts to Gladys Henry, in that hospital bed in Jacksonville, surrounded by family.

"My grandmother, the woman who made me who I am today, I want to thank you so much," Henry said. "Even though you can't be here today, I feel you in spirit, and I love you so much. . . . You always told me, 'Always keep God first, pray,' and that I'd always

Derrick Henry interviewed by reporters after a game at Bryant-Denny Stadium. (Photo by Mark Mayfield)

make it far. I just want you to know how much I love you and I'm praying for you."

Henry went on to thank his teammates, especially his offensive line, and his coaches, telling Saban: "You're a loyal coach. You always challenge us. I just love you coach, man. Without you, I wouldn't be here today."

Henry would go on to play two more games at Alabama before he opted to enter the NFL draft early as a junior. He's now playing for the Tennessee Titans. At Alabama, he would leave with a national championship, two SEC titles, and his name all over the Alabama record books.

His performances against Michigan State and Clemson expanded his SEC single-season rushing record to 2,219 yards and 28 touchdowns. His 3,591 total career yards would also eclipse a school record, along with the 20 consecutive games in which he scored at least one touchdown.

Shortly before the Cotton Bowl battle with Michigan State, Alabama offensive coordinator Lane Kiffin was asked why Henry was having such a record-breaking year.

"None of us thought this was going to happen," Kiffin said. "It's two things. The first thing is Derrick. He's unique. They just don't make guys that big, that fast, that tough. They just don't. That's genetics and work ethic. The second thing was injuries to Kenyan Drake. And so, I don't think the numbers would be where they were had Kenyan not been injured. They'd still be up there, but I think there would be some balance in there."

As for all those carries for Henry, Kiffin said, "I was always a 20–25 carry [coach]. You worry about ball security because that's where the fumbles increase. And so it just blows me away sometimes. I ask them upstairs on the headset, where he's [Henry's] at. He's at 30, he's at 36, at 38 carries, but it doesn't seem like it. It doesn't even seem like you're giving

Part Five

him the ball that much. It doesn't seem like he's wearing down. You're down there to see the body language and to see where he is. We both [Saban and Kiffin] talk all the time about taking him out, but no reason to."

Indeed. As Henry had said after carrying the ball 46 times for 271 yards in Alabama's 29–13 victory over Auburn: "The ball isn't that heavy, so I was good."

37

Back On Top

It had not always been this way. This national stage.

When Nick Saban arrived in Tuscaloosa in 2007, Alabama had not won or even competed for a national championship since 1992—fifteen long years for a proud program, but one mired in the past, suffering through NCAA sanctions, and miserably confined to mostly minor bowls.

But that all changed, and quickly. Saban's Alabama teams had now won three BCS national championships and four SEC titles since 2009 and were once again back in their familiar spotlight on the game's biggest stage. But this was different. The BCS was gone, replaced by the College Football Playoff at the end of the 2014 season. And now, on January 11, 2016, Alabama was set to play Clemson in only the second-ever CFP national championship game. Both teams had won semifinal contests in dominating fashion twelve days earlier. (The Tide had blown out Michigan State 38–0 in the Cotton Bowl and Clemson had rolled over Oklahoma 37–17 in the Orange Bowl.)

Now the Tide and Tigers would meet at University of Phoenix Stadium in Glendale, Arizona. It would be an evening to remember.

While many college football analysts were picking Clemson, the oddsmakers in Las Vegas were not. Alabama opened as a 7-point favorite. That did not sit well with Clemson players and their coaches. After all, Clemson was the No. 1 team in America, with a record of 14–0, and riding a 17-game winning streak, the longest in the nation. The Crimson Tide was 13–1, having lost in a turnover-filled upset to Ole Miss in the third game of the season before reeling off 11 consecutive victories.

"Well, I mean, the message there is just, you know, we may not be the favorite, but we don't see ourselves as an underdog," Tigers coach Dabo Swinney said two days before the game. "We think that we've got a great team, and I think that our guys have done a great

Part Five

Cyrus Jones returns a punt 69 yards for a touchdown against Mississippi State on November 14, 2015. (Photo by Layton Dudley/*The Crimson White*, courtesy of the UA Office of Student Media)

job of embracing every role that we've been put in for the last seven years, to be honest with you. That's why we've been so consistent."

No matter the betting line, it was evident there was a mutual respect between the two national championship contenders. Even Alabama fans found it hard to work up a good dislike for Dabo Swinney, and there was good reason for it. Swinney was a former Alabama receiver and special teams player who had been a member of that 1992 national championship team, the one that destroyed undefeated and favored Miami 34–13 in the Sugar Bowl.

But Swinney wasn't just any player. He had to earn his way. A native of Pelham, Alabama, Swinney joined the Crimson Tide as a walk-on, later received a scholarship, and lettered three years in a row. He became the first person in his family to graduate from college, got an MBA in Tuscaloosa, then served as an assistant coach for the Crimson Tide's Gene Stallings.

Such deep ties made the upcoming contest difficult for some of Swinney's former teammates and friends in Alabama. Asked what he had heard from them, Swinney deftly answered, "A lot of them are just saying, well, 'Good luck to you,' or they're saying, 'Hey,

I'm pulling for you. You're my brother, you're my relationship. But don't tell anybody.' So I've had a little bit of everything, but it's fun. There will be a lot of people happy one way or another Monday night."

Still, Swinney added: "You know, to be able to be in my first national championship and beat The University of Alabama, where I won a national championship, would be pretty special."

The mutual admiration extended to the players, including the teams' two biggest stars, Clemson's Deshaun Watson and Alabama's Derrick Henry.

"We spent a lot of time together in New York at the Heisman ceremony," Henry said. "Deshaun is a really good person. I could see the motivation that he carries with him to be a good person. He works hard at both being a good athlete as well as a good person. I gained a lot of respect for him."

But now there was a game to play and trophy to be awarded.

The stakes were high, as Clemson, the higher seed in their home orange, and Alabama in visiting whites, took the field on a magical night in Arizona. ESPN and ABC play-by-play announcer Chris Fowler set the tone, and the stakes, at least for Alabama: "Nick Saban told his team, 'You deserve to be here, but you're entitled to nothing.' Anything less than a victory tonight and this season ends in disappointment for Bama."

Both Clemson and Alabama had won their semifinal matchups in blowouts, but this would be a titanic, dazzling battle that would go back and forth until one team, the Crimson Tide, took one of the gutsiest risks ever in a championship game—a stunningly successful onside kick in the fourth quarter—and the other, the Tigers, ran out of time after fighting to the end. When it was over, Alabama's 45–40 victory would earn the program its fourth national championship in seven years—a dynasty by any measure—and Nick Saban his fifth national title, putting him squarely in the sights of Paul "Bear" Bryant's record six championships.

This was, indeed, a game for the ages, one that delivered from almost the very beginning. Midway through the first quarter. Alabama's Alphonse Taylor, Dominick Jackson, and O. J. Howard opened a hole so massive on the right side of the line that Henry looked like the proverbial Mack truck rushing through it on his way to a 50-yard touchdown. It was the first big play in a game of big plays.

Howard, the big tight end who had been used sparingly as a receiver up until the Michigan State game, would do far more than block on this night. In the third quarter, he caught his first touchdown pass of the season, taking advantage of blown coverage by Clemson for a 53-yard score down the sideline. He added another spectacular score in the fourth quarter, again running past Clemson's coverage, splitting the field and catching a perfectly thrown pass from Jake Coker for 51 yards and a touchdown. Howard would be named the game's most valuable offensive player, with 208 receiving yards and two touchdowns on just five catches.

Even Saban acknowledged after the game that Howard, with such enormous talent, should have had more touches in earlier games.

"Well, O. J., quite honestly, should have been more involved all year long," Saban said. "Sometimes he was open and we didn't get him the ball, but I think the last two games have been breakout games for him in terms of what he is capable of, and what he can do. I would say that it's bad coaching on my part that he didn't have the opportunity to do that all year long, because he really is a good athlete, and he's improved tremendously as a player this year."

A week later, Howard, a junior eligible to declare for the NFL draft, rewarded his coach's support by agreeing to return for his senior year at Alabama.

For now, next season could wait. It was time for celebration.

"This is what we stood up and said at the beginning of the season. We wanted to come out and win a national championship this season, and our team fought hard for that," Howard said. "And I'm just so proud of our team, and no team deserved this more than we do."

Henry also had another big night, rushing for 158 yards and three touchdowns on 36 carries. It was his tenth 100-plus-yards rushing game of the season and left him with 2,219 total yards and 28 touchdowns rushing, both Alabama and SEC records. It also marked his 20th consecutive game with a touchdown, the longest streak in the nation.

But the touchdowns from both Henry and Howard, and an exemplary second half from Coker (who threw for a career-high 335 yards and two touchdowns) were still not enough, together, to put away Clemson. It took a full team effort in all three phases of the game: offense, defense, and special teams. Especially with a nearly superhuman performance on the field from Clemson's Deshaun Watson, a dual-threat quarterback who threw for 405 yards and four touchdowns, and rushed for 73 more yards against the nation's best defense.

Watson did everything he could in a masterful performance, buying himself time against Alabama's rush and making plenty of pinpoint throws. But in the end, he said he could have done more.

"Going into this game, I was expecting to win," he said. "I thought we should have won. But like coach Swinney said, there were a few plays that we didn't really capitalize on, and I missed some throws. We dropped some balls and just had some miscues. Just some little things like that is going to really force yourself into a hole, and it's hard to beat a team like Alabama if you make those mistakes."

There was nothing Watson personally could have done to stop what became the turning point in the game, with 10:34 left in the fourth quarter.

Alabama had just tied the game at 24–24 with a 33-yard Adam Griffith field goal. Griffith and his teammates lined up for what appeared to be a normal kickoff. Clemson's front line pinched over closer to one side of the field, anticipating that Griffith would kick it deep toward the corner, as he had routinely done. The Tigers' formation left an opening on the other side of the field, a formation Alabama had seen earlier in the game and had also studied on Clemson game films.

Alabama had practiced for this moment.

With the go-ahead from Saban, Griffith executed a pop kick perfectly into the open space 15 yards downfield on the far side, and the Crimson Tide's Marlon Humphrey ran under it, catching it at midfield. The onside kick had completely caught Clemson by surprise and even elicited a rare grin from Saban on the sideline. The "Tide," quite literally, had just turned in the game.

Two plays later, Coker found Howard wide open down the middle of the field for that 51-yard touchdown, and Alabama had a lead at 31–24 that it would never relinquish, though there was plenty of scoring yet to come.

"That onside kick was a big momentum swing for our team," Howard said. "It got the sidelined energized. Everybody was pumped up, and we went down and scored on the next drive."

The gutsy call by Saban endeared him even more to a team that already would run through walls for him, and it underscored a major point: that even with as much success as Saban has had, he was willing to do something no one expected from him to get the edge in a tight game. Of course, it wasn't luck. His team, as always, had meticulously prepared. Part of the process.

"I put my trust in coach Saban 100 percent," said Bama safety Eddie Jackson, who had a key second-quarter interception and was named the game's most valuable defensive player. "I wouldn't want to be no other place and play for no other coach than coach Saban. He's a great coach, he's a great mentor, and he always leads us in the right direction."

Saban said he pulled the trigger on the kick, knowing Alabama needed a lift and his defense needed a rest.

"I thought we had it in the game any time we wanted to do it," Saban said. "I made the decision to do it because the game was tied 21–21 [actually 24–24] and we were tired on defense and weren't doing a great job of getting them stopped. And I felt like if we didn't change, do something, or take a chance to change the momentum of the game, that we wouldn't have a chance to win."

Swinney, who argued vehemently on the sideline even though the kick went 15 yards (only 10 was necessary) and Alabama wasn't offsides, gave credit where it was due after the game.

"It was a great kick," Swinney said. "First of all, he put it right in a good spot, and their kid did a great job of going and getting it. It was a huge play."

Ironically, Swinney and Clemson had used their own trickery, a successful fake punt, against Oklahoma in the Orange Bowl. But this was Alabama's night.

Still, it wasn't over.

Leading 31–27 after a Clemson field goal with 7:47 left in the game, the Crimson Tide's Kenyan Drake took the kickoff, ran toward the opposite side of the field, and sped 95 yards for a touchdown, diving the last four yards into the pylon at the front corner of the end zone. An extra point extended Alabama's lead to 11 points at 38–27, and some breathing room.

But Watson and his offense came right back again, driving 75 yards for a score to cut it to 38–33, and a chance to steal the momentum. But once again, Howard stepped up with a huge play, this time taking a short pass from Coker behind the line of scrimmage, cutting around the corner, and running 63 yards for a first down at the Clemson 14-yard line. It took six more plays, including a clutch three-yard run from Coker for a first down, and Henry finally managed to score on a third and goal from the Tigers' 1.

The lead was now 45–33 with just over a minute left. Watson, however, still wasn't finished. He drove his team downfield, scoring on a 24-yard pass to tight end Jordan Leggett. But an onside kick, with just 12 seconds left, went out of bounds, caught by the Tide's ArDarius Stewart anyway, and an instant classic of a championship game was finally over.

"They [Clemson] were real strong. Never quit, either," Jake Coker said after the game. "I have a lot of respect for them after this game. They were real similar to us. Got a lot of fight in them. Great program. They just do things the right way. Either team could have won. It's just we happened to make more plays later on in the game."

Minutes after he and his team accepted the College Football Playoff National Championship Trophy, Saban reflected back on this team. Always careful not to play favorites, the coach nevertheless made it clear this championship and this team was different, in some fundamental way.

"I really wanted to do the best I could for this team, probably as much as any team I've ever coached, because I really did want them to have the opportunity to win this game," the coach said. "We didn't always play pretty in this game. It probably wasn't one of our best games when it comes down to flat execution. But when it comes to competing and making plays when we needed to make them, it was probably as good as it gets."

Saban should know. The man had just won his fifth national championship, four with Alabama. And the only coach who had more was a guy whose statue stands very near Saban's own on the Walk of Champions at the north entrance to Bryant-Denny Stadium in Tuscaloosa. In another two years, that would change, too. Nick Saban was not done winning national titles at Alabama.

38

The Dynasty Rolls On

A modern new rivalry of elite-level football began playing out between Alabama and Clemson even as the Crimson Tide celebrated its thrilling victory over the Tigers in the 2016 CFB National Championship Game. A year later, both teams would be back in the final game again, producing another instant classic with a different outcome: Clemson won it 35–31 on a Deshaun Watson to Hunter Renfrow touchdown pass with just one second left on the clock in Tampa, Florida's, Raymond James Stadium.

It was a heartbreaking defeat for Alabama, but the "process" that Nick Saban had installed a decade earlier in Tuscaloosa was not about one game. Dabo Swinney, Clemson's coach, was building his program for the long haul, as well. So history was not done with these two teams. They would both meet again for a third time in three years—this one in the CFP semifinal at the Sugar Bowl in New Orleans on New Year's Day 2018. But unlike the previous two meetings, where the outcome was not decided until the final seconds, there would be no late fourth quarter drama. Alabama, on the strength of an outstanding defensive performance, won this one 24–6 to advance to the national championship game for a third consecutive year.

Bama's opponent in the 2018 CFB National Championship Game would be the Georgia Bulldogs, setting up an all-SEC national title battle for the first time since Alabama routed LSU 21–0 to win the 2011 national championship. That game had been played under a different set of rankings—the Bowl Championship Series, a system that chose the final two teams based on two polls and six different computer rankings.

That had all changed with the beginning of the College Football Playoff at the end of the 2014 season. The new system included a four-team playoff, based on the final rankings of a select CFP committee each year. Alabama had made the playoff in each of the first three years the system existed and now was back for a fourth time, despite the fact that the previously unbeaten and injury-riddled Tide had lost in an upset at Auburn to end the 2017 season. No matter that one loss, Alabama—at 11–1—made the playoffs with the No. 4 ranking. It underscored the selection committee's mantra to choose the four best teams, no matter the conferences.

The other three playoff teams included No. 1 Clemson, No. 2 Oklahoma, and No. 3 Georgia. And following Bama's 24–6 victory over Clemson, and Georgia's wild 54–48 overtime win over Oklahoma, the stage was set for a thrilling final game in Atlanta's new Mercedes-Benz Stadium.

Georgia had not won a national championship since the days of Herschel Walker in 1980, so if ever a team was motivated, the Bulldogs were it. Alabama, by glaring contrast, had won four national championships in the past eight years.

For a while, it looked like all those years of pent-up frustration for Georgia were coming to an end. In their semifinal at the Rose Bowl, the Bulldogs had put up 527 total yards against Oklahoma, including 317 on the ground, with sensational running backs Nick Chubb and Sony Michel leading the way. It had been a masterful come-from-behind offensive performance. Now, in the national championship game against Alabama on the night of January 8, 2018, the Bulldogs jumped out to a 13–0 halftime lead. While Alabama's offense was struggling mightily, the defense, led by Mack Wilson, Rashaan Evans, Terrell Lewis, Minkah Fitzpatrick, Da'Ron Payne, Ronnie Harrison, and others, was preventing Georgia from blowing the game open.

Then came a Nick Saban decision that would change everything. Jalen Hurts had won 25 games and only lost two as Alabama's two-year starting quarterback. But seeing him struggle to complete passes in the first half, Saban made a switch, sending in freshman Tua Tagovailoa to start the third quarter. It was a gutsy call and it worked. Alabama rallied but still trailed Georgia 20–13 when—on a fourth-and-goal from the 7-yard line—Tagovailoa threw a bullet through traffic to Calvin Ridley in the end zone for a touchdown. An extra point tied the game at 20 all with 3:49 left.

One series later, the Tide had a chance to win it with just three seconds left in regulation, but Andy Pappanastos's 36-yard field goal attempt hooked left. Bama fans couldn't have known it at the time, but that simply made what was to come later even more dramatic.

Georgia had the ball first in overtime but went backwards when Bama's Terrell Lewis sacked quarterback Jake Fromm for a 13-yard loss. UGA placekicker Rodrigo Blankenship saved the Bulldogs, or so it seemed, with a 51-yard field goal. Now it was Alabama's turn, and it didn't start well, to say the least. Rather than throwing the ball away under the pressure from Georgia's pass rush, Tagovailoa was sacked for a loss of 16 yards at the Tide 41-yard line.

Alabama freshman quarterback Tua Tagovailoa throws a perfect 41-yard touchdown pass to DeVonta Smith, also a freshman, to win the 2018 College Football Playoff National Championship Game. (Photos by Sam MacDonald/*The Crimson White*, courtesy of the UA Office of Student Media)

Facing a daunting second-and-26, Tagovailoa dropped back again to pass, while another Tide freshman, DeVonta Smith, bolted down the sidelines behind Georgia defenders. Tagovailoa looked off a Georgia safety, freezing him in position across the middle of the field, then turned and launched a perfect strike to Smith, who caught it in full stride at the 1-yard line and raced into the end zone. It was a stunning, walk-off 41-yard touchdown, giving Alabama a 26–23 victory and the Tide's fifth national championship in nine years.

"Who would have ever thought I would have been here right now, in this moment?" Tagovailoa, from Hawaii, said during an ESPN interview after the game. "I thank God for that."

With the victory, Nick Saban won his sixth national championship, tying Paul Bryant for the most ever in college football. In his eleven seasons at Alabama, Saban now has a 132–20 record—an astonishing .868 winning percentage. But just as important in Saban's process, Alabama teams have won off the field, with a skyrocketing graduation rate since his arrival in 2007. The academic success of Saban's teams is often overshadowed by the championships. Both, however, are part of a dynasty that, as the fall of 2018 approached, showed no signs of slowing down.

Acknowledgments

The University of Alabama's football program is so steeped in history that no one book could do it justice. It is a story of thrilling victories, of furious comebacks, of dominant performances, of overcoming adversity, of singular moments, and of record-breaking seasons. It is also, as any honest history must be, a story of games that didn't break Alabama's way, of heroic efforts that came up short, of gut-wrenching losses. By far, however, it is the story of winning—and the Alabama Crimson Tide has been winning for a very long time. The simple truth is that no college football program in America has been winning championships so consistently, for so long, as Alabama.

It is a privilege to be able to tell some of these great stories. For me personally, the chapters about Paul "Bear" Bryant's era in Tuscaloosa brought back some wonderful memories. I had the opportunity to interview Bryant on several occasions during my time as sports editor and then editor-in-chief of UA's student newspaper, *The Crimson White*. But it was my last meeting with him, after graduation, that I've cherished the most. It was on a painfully cold February day in 1979, and I had returned to campus to interview him for an off-season story.

Bryant's wife, Mary Harmon, had been admitted to the hospital, and he was going to see her as soon as our meeting was over. So after the interview, he walked out with me toward the parking lot. It had starting snowing outside, a rare event in Tuscaloosa. As I turned to head toward my car, he told me, "Son, I know you're a southerner and I know you don't know how to drive in this stuff any more than I do. Be careful now."

In that moment, he seemed more like a grandfather than the most famous football coach in America. I wouldn't trade anything for that. Nearly four years later, I was working at *USA Today* in northern Virginia when I got word that Bryant had died suddenly of a heart attack. I recall my colleagues surrounding me at my desk, offering condolences as if a member of my family had died. And in many ways, that's exactly how it felt. And I wasn't alone. University of Alabama alums, along with countless other Bama fans who never attended the school, felt like they had lost a close friend.

Bryant gave us so many great Alabama football moments worth remembering. Hopefully this book does justice to some of those, along with so many others in this program. And as we all know, coach Nick Saban and his teams have taken Crimson Tide football to even greater heights in the past decade. As this book underscores, Alabama has had a tradition of success throughout the decades, but we are currently witnessing a dynasty that is unprecedented in modern football.

Throughout my career, I have been inspired and influenced by far too many people to name here. But I could never write a book without thinking how fortunate I've been to have such a supporting family. My children Matt, Stephanie, Madison, and Alexa, and Steph's three fabulous boys, my grandkids, Kip, Hayes, and Graham, are a great inspiration, always. My wife, Monica, spent many nights helping edit these pages, and keeping the manuscript on track. Thanks also to the heroes of my life, my parents, Dewey and Phyllis Mayfield. There are simply no better people on this planet than Mom and Dad.

No Alabama history book could be complete without a visit to the Paul W. Bryant Museum in Tuscaloosa, and I'm indebted to director Ken Gaddy for his expertise and help. Thanks, as well, to my longtime friend Tommy Ford, an associate athletics director at UA and author of so many books on the Crimson Tide that I've lost count. Tommy's love for Bama football, combined with his writing talent, have been a great asset to the university and to Crimson Tide fans everywhere.

It has been a pleasure these last few years to work at UA, and most especially to work around some truly talented students. Some of the outstanding images accompanying this book were taken by our student photographers at *The Crimson White*, where I serve as editorial adviser. They include Layton Dudley, Pete Pajor, Sam MacDonald, Drew Hoover, Austin Bigoney, and John Michael Simpson, among others. Thanks, as well, to Paul Wright, director of Student Media at UA, who has created an environment of training, learning, and support that will benefit our student journalists well into their professional careers.

I can't write a book about Bama football without also mentioning Dr. Adam Sterritt and Andrew Deere, who cohost a weekly football show with me each fall on 90.7 The Capstone, the campus radio station. We call it *Skybox*, and it's a show in which we make weekly game picks and interview guests—including former Bama players, Crimson Tide beat reporters, local officials, and, quite often, the good folks in the division in which we work at UA—Student Life. Terry Siggers, general manager of the station, produces the show for us and has saved the day more than once by correcting our technical glitches. I can't mention *Skybox* without also pointing out that our former UA colleague, Dr. George Brown, helped create the show and continues to pick games with us from afar . . . that would be from his position now as assistant vice provost and director of recreation and wellness at The University of Minnesota-Twin Cities.

As for the game picks . . . well . . . we all get one or two right every now and then.

Thanks, as well, to my friend Jim Rainey, publisher of *The Tuscaloosa News*, an outstanding source for University of Alabama sports coverage. And thanks, as always, to The University of Alabama Athletics Communications Office, clearly one of the best sports information offices in the nation

Finally, and importantly, a debt of gratitude to Julie Ganz, editorial director for sports at Skyhorse Publishing in New York, and former Skyhorse senior editor Ken Samelson, for their guidance and editing. I appreciate their professionalism and commitment to this book.

—Mark Mayfield
April 30, 2018
Tuscaloosa, Alabama

References

Bibliography

Barra, Allen. (2005). *The Last Coach: A life of Paul "Bear" Bryant*. New York, NY: W. W. Norton & Company.

Berkow, Ira. (2001, October 29). Sports of the Times; A Towering Man in Alabama. *The New York Times*. Retrieved at nytimes.com.

Bernstein, Rick, & Sabol, Steve (Producers). Shapiro, Ouisie (Writer). (2012). *Namath: From Beaver Falls to Broadway* [Documentary film]. New York, NY: HBO & NFL Films.

Browning, Al. (1992). *Bowl Bama Bowl* (4th ed.). Nashville, TN: Rutledge Hill Press.

Browning, Al. (2002). *I Remember Paul "Bear" Bryant*. Nashville, TN: Cumberland Press.

Bryant, Paul W., & Underwood, John. (1974). *Bear: The Hard Life and Good Times of Alabama's Coach Bryant*. Boston, MA: Little, Brown and Company.

Burke, Monte. (2015). *Nick Saban: The Making of a Coach*. New York, NY: Simon & Schuster.

Cook, Ben, & Wells, Lawrence. (1982). *Legend in Crimson: A Photo History of Alabama Football*. Oxford, MS: Sports Yearbook Company/Yoknapatawpha Press.

Copeland, Bobby J. (2005). *Johnny Mack Brown: Up Close and Personal*. Madison, NC: Empire Publishing.

Crider, Beverly. (2013). *Lost Birmingham*. Charleston, SC: The History Press.

Dunnavant, Keith. (1996). *Coach: The Life of Paul "Bear" Bryant*. New York, NY: Simon & Schuster.

Dunnavant, Keith. (2006). *The Missing Ring: How Bear Bryant and the 1966 Alabama Crimson Tide Were Denied College Football's Most Elusive Prize*. New York, NY: Thomas Dunne Books.

Edson, James, S. (1946). *Alabama's Crimson Tide 1892–1945*. Montgomery, AL: The Paragon Press.

Ford, Tommy. (2012). *Tornado to National Title # 14: The Story Behind the National Championship Year*. Atlanta, GA: Whitman Publishing.

Ford, Tommy, & Mayfield, Mark. (2013). *Crimson Domination: The Process Behind Alabama's 15th National Championship*. Atlanta, GA: Whitman Publishing.

Ford, Tommy. (2017). *The University of Alabama Football Vault* (3rd ed.). Atlanta, GA: Whitman Publishing.

Gaddy, Ken. (2017). *Sixteen and Counting: The National Championships of Alabama Football*. Tuscaloosa, AL: The University of Alabama Press.

Graham, Frank, Jr. (1963, March 23). The story of a College Football Fix. *The Saturday Evening Post*, 80–83.

Greenburg, Ross (Producer). (2013). *Against the Tide* [Documentary film]. United States: Showtime Networks.

Greene, Bob. (2018, January 5). The University of Alabama Earns a Victory over an Ugly History. *The Wall Street Journal*. Retrieved at wsj.com.

Hamner, Thomas J. Jr. (1997). *Strike Up The Million Dollar Band 1912–1935: A History of the Early Years of the University of Alabama's band*. Tuscaloosa, AL: Self-published.

Hemphill, Paul. (1993). *Leaving Birmingham: Notes of a Native Son*. New York, NY: Viking.

Houlgate, Deke. (1954). *The Football Thesaurus: 85 Years on the American Gridiron*. Los Angeles, CA: Houlgate House.

Housel, David, & Ford, Tommy. (2009). *Alabama-Auburn Rivalry Football Vault*. Atlanta, GA: Whitman Publishing.

Kirby, James. (1986). *Fumble: Bear Bryant, Wally Butts, and the Great College Football Scandal*. New York, NY: Harcourt Brace Jovanovich.

Mayfield, Mark. (2016). *Back on Top! The Alabama Crimson Tide's 2015–2016 Championship Football Season*. New York, NY: Sports Publishing/Skyhorse Publishing.

Namath, Joe. (2006). *Namath*. New York, NY: Rugged Land.

Roberts, Randy, & Krzemienski, Ed. (2013). *Rising Tide: Bear Bryant, Joe Namath & Dixie's Last Quarter*. New York, NY: Twelve/Hachette Book Group.

Schor, Gene. (1991). *100 Years of Alabama Football*. Atlanta, GA: Longstreet Press.

Scott, Richard, with Mayfield, Jason. (2014). *Legends of Alabama Football* (2nd ed.). New York, NY: Sports Publishing/Skyhorse Publishing.

Sellers, James B. (2014). *History of the University of Alabama: Volume One 1818–1902*. Tuscaloosa, AL: The University of Alabama Press.

Stabler, Ken, & Stainback, Berry. (1986). *Snake: The Candid Life of Football's Most Outrageous Renegade*. Garden City, NY: Doubleday & Company.

Stephenson, Creg, & McNair, Kirk. (2011). *Always a Crimson Tide: Players, Coaches, and Fans Share Their Passion for Alabama Football*. Chicago, IL: Triumph Books.

Stoddard, Tom. (1996). *Turnaround: The Untold Story of Bear Bryant's First Year as Head Coach at Alabama*. Montgomery, AL: Black Belt Press.

Sulzby, James F. (1960). *Historic Alabama Hotels and Resorts*. Tuscaloosa, AL: The University of Alabama Press.

Underwood, John. (1965, January 11). Fabulous in Defeat. *Sports Illustrated*. (22)2, 14–17.

Whittington, Richard. (2001). *Rites of Autumn: The Story of College Football*. New York, NY: The Free Press.

Institutional/Public Research Sources

The Birmingham Public Library

The Paul W. Bryant Museum

The University of Alabama Athletics Communications Office

The University of Alabama Libraries

The University of Alabama Office of Student Media

The University of Pennsylvania Archives & Records Center

Media sources

247Sports/BamaOnline

ABC Sports

Alabama Media Group

CBS Sports

Crimson magazine

ESPN

HBO

NBC Sports

SEC Country

Showtime Networks

Sports Illustrated

The Anniston Star

The Associated Press

The Atlanta Journal-Constitution

The Birmingham News

The Crimson White
The Los Angeles Times
The New York Times
The Philadelphia Inquirer
The Seattle Times
The Tuscaloosa News
The Wall Street Journal
The Washington Post
WVUA-FM/90.7 The Capstone